Preface

Welcome to " Microsoft Azure Interview Questions and Answers " a comprehensive guide designed to help you prepare for interviews related to Microsoft Azure, one of the leading cloud computing platforms in the industry. Whether you are a seasoned Azure professional looking to brush up on your knowledge or a newcomer eager to explore the world of Azure, this guide will prove to be an invaluable resource. Why Azure? As organizations increasingly embrace the cloud to meet their computing and data storage needs, Azure has emerged as a powerful and versatile platform that offers a wide array of services and solutions. Whether you are interested in infrastructure as a service (IaaS), platform as a service (PaaS), or software as a service (SaaS), Azure has you covered. Azure's global presence, scalability, robust security features, and extensive ecosystem make it a top choice for businesses of all sizes. Interviews for Azure-related roles can be challenging and competitive, requiring a deep understanding of Azure's services, architecture, best practices, and real-world applications.

Comprehensive Coverage: This guide covers a wide range of Azure topics, from the fundamentals to advanced concepts. Whether you are facing a technical interview or a discussion about Azure's strategic impact on an organization, you'll find relevant content here. Interview-Ready Questions: Resources: Throughout the guide, we provide links to additional resources, documentation, and Azure services that can help you further explore the topics discussed.

This guide is structured into chapters, each focusing on a specific aspect of Azure. Feel free to navigate to the sections that align with your current level of expertise or areas you wish to improve. Whether you are a beginner looking to build a strong foundation or an experienced Azure architect seeking to refine your knowledge, there is something here for you.

Table of Contents

Chapter 1: Introduction to Microsoft Azure

1.1 Getting Started with Microsoft Azure

1.1.1 What is Microsoft Azure, and why is it significant in the world of cloud computing?
Microsoft Azure is a cloud computing platform and service offered by Microsoft. It's significant because it provides a vast range of cloud-based services, enabling organizations to build, deploy, and manage applications and infrastructure in a scalable and cost-effective manner.

1.1.2 How can someone create a Microsoft Azure account, and what are the key benefits of having one?
To create a Microsoft Azure account, individuals can sign up on the Azure website. Benefits include access to a wide array of Azure services, a free tier for experimentation, and the ability to leverage cloud resources for various purposes, such as development, testing, and production workloads.

1.1.3 What is the Azure Portal, and how does it serve as a central hub for Azure management?
The Azure Portal is a web-based interface that allows users to manage and monitor their Azure resources and services. It offers a user-friendly dashboard where you can create, configure, and monitor Azure resources, making it a central hub for Azure management.

1.1.4 What is an Azure subscription, and how does it relate to resource management in Azure?
An Azure subscription is a billing and management container used to provision and manage Azure resources. It serves as the billing entity and allows users to organize and control access to resources. Subscriptions help manage costs and enforce access control within an Azure environment.

1.1.5 Can you explain the concept of resource groups in Azure and their role in resource management?
Resource groups in Azure are logical containers that hold related Azure resources. They help organize and manage resources based on projects, departments, or environments. Resource groups simplify resource management by allowing users to apply policies, access control, and cost tracking to a group of related resources.

1.1.6 What role does Azure Active Directory (Azure AD) play in Azure, and how does it enhance security and identity management?
Azure AD is Microsoft's identity and access management service for the cloud. It provides secure authentication, single sign-on (SSO), and identity management for Azure services and applications, enhancing security and user experience.

1.1.7 What is Azure App Service, and why is it popular for hosting web and mobile applications?
Azure App Service is a platform for building, deploying, and scaling web and mobile applications. It simplifies application management tasks and offers features like automatic scaling, continuous integration, and integration with Azure DevOps.

1.1.8 How can Azure storage services like Azure Blob Storage and Azure Table Storage be used for data management in the cloud?
Azure Blob Storage is ideal for storing unstructured data like images and documents, while Azure Table Storage is a NoSQL data store for semi-structured datasets. Both services provide scalability and durability for data in the cloud.

1.1.9 What are Azure Resource Groups, and how do they help in organizing and managing Azure resources?

Azure Resource Groups are logical containers that hold related Azure resources. They simplify resource management, billing, and access control by allowing users to manage resources as a single unit.

1.1.10 What is the Azure Marketplace, and how can organizations benefit from it when deploying applications and services?

The Azure Marketplace is a catalog of pre-built applications and services that can be easily deployed in Azure. It accelerates application deployment, reduces development time, and offers a wide range of solutions from various vendors, simplifying resource provisioning and management.

1.2 Understanding Cloud Computing

1.2.1 What is cloud computing, and how does it differ from traditional on-premises IT infrastructure?

Cloud computing is a technology model that provides on-demand access to a shared pool of computing resources over the internet. It differs from traditional on-premises infrastructure in that it allows organizations to access and use resources like virtual machines, storage, and databases without the need for physical hardware or upfront capital investment. Cloud services are scalable, flexible, and often pay-as-you-go, making them more cost-effective and adaptable to changing needs.

1.2.2 What are the key service models in cloud computing, and how do they differ?

Cloud computing offers three primary service models: Infrastructure as a Service (IaaS), Platform as a Service (PaaS), and Software as a Service (SaaS). IaaS provides virtualized computing resources, PaaS offers a platform for application development, and SaaS delivers fully managed software applications. The key difference lies in the level of control and responsibility shared between the cloud provider and the user.

1.2.3 What are the benefits of cloud computing for businesses?

Cloud computing offers several benefits, including:

- Cost savings through reduced capital expenditure.
- Scalability to handle changing workloads.
- Accessibility from anywhere with an internet connection.
- Disaster recovery and data redundancy.
- Enhanced collaboration and productivity through cloud-based tools.

1.2.4 What are public, private, and hybrid clouds, and when might organizations choose one over the others?

- Public Cloud: Operated by cloud providers and accessible to the general public. Suitable for most workloads due to cost-effectiveness and scalability.
- Private Cloud: Dedicated to a single organization. Chosen for sensitive data or strict compliance requirements.
- Hybrid Cloud: Combines public and private clouds, offering flexibility, data residency requirements, and the ability to leverage existing infrastructure.

1.2.5 What is cloud security, and what are some key considerations for securing data and applications in the cloud?

Cloud security involves practices, technologies, and policies for protecting data, applications, and infrastructure in the cloud. Key considerations include identity and access management (IAM), encryption, network security, regular audits, and compliance with data protection regulations. Ensuring the security of cloud resources is essential for maintaining trust and data integrity.

1.2.6 What are the primary security concerns associated with cloud computing, and how can they be mitigated?

Security concerns include data breaches, data loss, and compliance. Mitigation strategies involve encryption, access control, regular audits, and compliance with industry regulations.

1.2.7 Explain the concept of cloud service-level agreements (SLAs) and their significance in cloud contracts.

Cloud SLAs define the terms of service, including uptime guarantees, performance expectations, and support levels. They are crucial for ensuring service reliability and accountability between cloud providers and customers.

1.2.8 What is cloud orchestration, and how does it streamline cloud management and provisioning?

Cloud orchestration is the automation of complex workflows and processes for provisioning, configuring, and managing cloud resources. It streamlines cloud management, reduces manual tasks, and enhances resource optimization.

1.2.9 What role does virtualization play in cloud computing, and how does it enable resource sharing?

Virtualization abstracts physical hardware into virtual machines (VMs) or containers, allowing multiple VMs to share the same physical resources. This enables efficient resource utilization and isolation.

1.2.10 How does cloud computing impact the scalability and availability of applications and services?

Cloud computing provides rapid elasticity, allowing applications to scale resources up or down based on demand. This scalability enhances availability and ensures that applications can handle varying workloads efficiently.

1.3 Introduction to Azure Services

1.3.1 What are Azure services, and how do they fit into Microsoft's cloud platform?

Azure services are a set of cloud computing offerings provided by Microsoft. They cover a wide range of capabilities, including computing, networking, storage, databases, AI, and more. These services are designed to help organizations build, deploy, and manage applications and infrastructure in the cloud, enabling scalability and cost-efficiency.

1.2.2 Can you differentiate between Azure Infrastructure as a Service (IaaS) and Azure Platform as a Service (PaaS) offerings?

Azure IaaS: Provides virtualized computing resources, where users manage the operating system and applications. Examples include Azure Virtual Machines (VMs).

Azure PaaS: Offers a platform and runtime environment for application development, abstracting the underlying infrastructure. Examples include Azure App Service and Azure SQL Database.

1.3.3 What is the Azure Marketplace, and how can organizations benefit from it?

The Azure Marketplace is an online store that offers a wide variety of third-party applications, services, and solutions that are compatible with Azure. Organizations can benefit from it by finding pre-built solutions, templates, and consulting services that accelerate application development and deployment in Azure.

1.3.4 How does Azure support hybrid cloud scenarios, and what are the advantages of such a setup?

Azure provides services and solutions for hybrid cloud scenarios, allowing organizations to seamlessly connect on-premises infrastructure with Azure resources. The advantages include flexibility in workload placement, data residency compliance, and the ability to leverage existing investments while taking advantage of cloud benefits.

1.3.5 What are some common Azure services used for data storage and management, and in what scenarios are they typically applied?

Common Azure services for data storage and management include Azure Blob Storage for unstructured data, Azure SQL Database for relational data, Azure Cosmos DB for NoSQL data, and Azure Data Lake Storage for big data analytics. These services are applied in various scenarios, from web applications to data warehousing and IoT solutions.

1.3.6 What is Azure App Service, and what types of applications can be hosted on it?

Azure App Service is a platform for building, deploying, and scaling web and mobile applications. It supports web apps, APIs, and mobile app backends, making it versatile for a wide range of application types.

1.3.7 How does Azure Active Directory (Azure AD) enhance identity and access management in Azure services?

Azure AD is Microsoft's identity and access management service for the cloud. It provides secure authentication, single sign-on (SSO), and access control to Azure services and applications, enhancing security and user experience.

1.3.8 What are Azure Functions, and what are some common use cases for serverless computing?

Azure Functions is a serverless compute service that allows developers to run code in response to events. Common use cases include event-driven applications, data processing, and automation.

1.3.9 How does Azure Storage facilitate data storage in the cloud, and what are its primary storage types?

Azure Storage offers scalable, secure, and highly available data storage options. Its primary storage types include Azure Blob Storage, Azure Table Storage, Azure Queue Storage, and Azure File Storage, each designed for specific data storage needs.

1.4 Creating an Azure Account

1.4.1. What is the process for creating a Microsoft Azure account, and is there a cost associated with it?

To create a Microsoft Azure account, individuals can visit the Azure website and sign up. There is no cost associated with creating an Azure account, and users are typically offered a free trial with a credit to explore Azure services.

1.4.2 What information and details are required during the Azure account creation process?

During Azure account creation, users are typically required to provide their contact information, such as name, email address, and phone number. Additionally, they need to set up a username and password for their Azure account.

1.4.3 Can you explain the difference between a Microsoft account and an Azure account?

A Microsoft account (e.g., Outlook or Hotmail) is a general-purpose account used for various Microsoft services, while an Azure account is specifically for accessing and managing Microsoft Azure cloud services. Users can use their Microsoft account to sign up for an Azure account.

1.4.4What is the purpose of the Azure subscription, and how does it affect resource management within Azure?

An Azure subscription is a billing and management container for Azure resources. It serves as the billing entity and allows users to organize, control access, and manage costs for Azure resources. Different subscriptions can have different access controls and billing setups.

1.4.5 What are some best practices for securing and managing an Azure account once it's created?

Best practices include enabling multi-factor authentication (MFA) for added security, regularly reviewing and managing access permissions, setting up budget alerts to monitor costs, and following Azure's recommendations for securing resources. Keeping account credentials secure is essential to prevent unauthorized access.

1.4.6 What is the Azure Portal, and how can users access and manage their Azure resources through it?

The Azure Portal is a web-based interface for managing Azure resources. Users can access it through a web browser to create, configure, and monitor Azure resources.

1.4.7 What is Azure Active Directory (Azure AD), and how does it relate to Azure account creation?

Azure AD is Microsoft's cloud-based identity and access management service. It is used to authenticate and authorize users for Azure services and resources, making it an integral part of Azure account creation and management.

1.4.8 Can an Azure subscription be associated with multiple Azure accounts, and how does role-based access control (RBAC) work in this context?

Yes, an Azure subscription can be associated with multiple Azure accounts. RBAC allows users to assign roles and permissions to specific individuals or groups, granting or limiting access to Azure resources within the subscription.

1.4.9 What are the best practices for securing an Azure account and ensuring data protection?

Best practices include enabling multi-factor authentication (MFA), using strong passwords, implementing access control with RBAC, auditing and monitoring account activities, and regularly reviewing and updating security policies.

ONLINE RESOURCES

Practice Paper

Link : https://forms.gle/yamVxV4NoQj7A8H47

QR Code :

Video Content

Link :

https://www.youtube.com/playlist?list=PLzlh_31VWEFoGhUkxGinUoUfYzHxGWEd6

QR Code :

Chapter 2: Azure Portal and Management Tools

2.1 Exploring the Azure Portal

2.1.1 What is the Azure Portal, and how does it serve as a central interface for managing Azure resources?

The Azure Portal is a web-based interface that provides a unified and user-friendly dashboard for managing Azure resources and services. It offers a single point of access to create, configure, and monitor Azure resources, making it a central hub for Azure management.

2.1.2 Can you explain the concept of Azure Resource Groups, and how are they used within the Azure Portal?

Azure Resource Groups are logical containers that hold related Azure resources. In the Azure Portal, they help users organize and manage resources by grouping them together based on projects, departments, or environments. Resource Groups simplify resource management and allow users to apply policies and access control to a set of related resources.

2.1.3 What is the Azure Marketplace, and how can users leverage it through the Azure Portal?

The Azure Marketplace is an online store that offers a wide variety of third-party applications, services, and solutions that are compatible with Azure. Users can access and deploy these solutions directly from the Azure Portal. It provides a convenient way to find and deploy pre-built solutions to enhance Azure services.

2.1.4 How does the Azure Portal facilitate role-based access control (RBAC) and user management within Azure environments?

The Azure Portal provides RBAC capabilities, allowing administrators to assign specific roles and permissions to users and groups. Through the portal, administrators can grant or restrict access to Azure resources, ensuring that users have the appropriate level of access based on their roles and responsibilities.

2.1.5 What are Dashboards in the Azure Portal, and how can users customize them to meet their needs?

Dashboards in the Azure Portal are customizable, user-defined views that display key information and resources. Users can create their own dashboards, add tiles representing Azure resources and metrics, and arrange them to tailor the view to their specific needs. Dashboards provide a personalized and efficient way to monitor and manage Azure resources.

2.1.6 What are Azure Tags, and how can they be used to label and categorize resources in the Azure Portal?

Azure Tags are name-value pairs that can be assigned to resources. They help users categorize, organize, and track resources for billing, cost analysis, and management purposes in the portal.

2.1.7 How can users search for specific Azure resources and services efficiently within the Azure Portal?

Users can use the search bar at the top of the portal to find resources by name, type, or keyword. The search results provide quick access to relevant resources.

2.1.8 What is the Azure Marketplace, and how can users' access and deploy solutions from it through the Azure Portal?

The Azure Marketplace is a catalog of pre-built applications and services. Users can access it through the portal to discover, purchase, and deploy solutions directly into their Azure environment.

2.1.9 What role does the Azure Cloud Shell play in the Azure Portal, and how can it assist users with managing Azure resources?
Azure Cloud Shell is an integrated command-line interface (CLI) within the portal. It allows users to run Azure CLI or PowerShell commands directly from the portal, simplifying resource management and automation tasks.

2.2 Azure PowerShell and Azure CLI

2.2.1 What are Azure PowerShell and Azure CLI, and how do they differ in managing Azure resources?
Azure PowerShell and Azure CLI are command-line interfaces for interacting with Azure resources. Azure PowerShell is based on Windows PowerShell and is typically used on Windows systems, while Azure CLI is a cross-platform command-line tool that can be used on Windows, macOS, and Linux. Both tools allow users to manage Azure resources, but the choice between them often depends on personal preference and the operating system in use.
2.2.2 How do you authenticate and sign in to Azure using Azure PowerShell and Azure CLI?
• Azure PowerShell: You can use the Connect-AzAccount cmdlet to sign in. It will prompt you to enter your Azure credentials.
• Azure CLI: Use the az login command, and a web page will open in your default web browser to complete the authentication.
2.2.3 What are some common use cases for Azure PowerShell and Azure CLI when managing Azure resources?
Both tools are used for various tasks, including creating and configuring Azure resources, deploying applications, managing access control, and automating resource provisioning and scaling. Azure PowerShell is known for its rich scripting capabilities, while Azure CLI provides a simple, human-readable syntax.
2.2.4 How do Azure PowerShell and Azure CLI help with automation in Azure environments?
Azure PowerShell and Azure CLI support scripting and automation by allowing users to create and execute scripts to perform repetitive tasks. Users can write scripts to provision and configure resources, automate deployments, and schedule maintenance tasks, reducing manual effort and ensuring consistency.
2.2.5 Are there any best practices or considerations for choosing between Azure PowerShell and Azure CLI for specific tasks?
While both tools can accomplish the same tasks, consider the following:
• Use Azure PowerShell if you are comfortable with Windows PowerShell scripting and want a comprehensive set of Azure cmdlets.
• Use Azure CLI if you prefer a cross-platform tool that follows Unix-style conventions and is easily integrated into bash or other shell scripts.
• You can use both tools together in the same Azure environment, choosing the one that best suits your needs for a particular task.
2.2.6 How can you list and filter Azure resources using Azure PowerShell and Azure CLI?
In Azure PowerShell, you can use cmdlets like **Get-AZ Resource** and filter using the **-ResourceGroupName** parameter. In Azure CLI, you can use commands like **AZ resource list** and filter using the **--resource-group** option.
2.2.7 What are some common use cases for scripting and automation with Azure PowerShell or Azure CLI?

Common use cases include provisioning and configuring resources, setting up deployment pipelines, automating backup and maintenance tasks, and managing resources across multiple Azure subscriptions.

2.2.8 How can you update and delete Azure resources using Azure PowerShell or Azure CLI?

Answer: You can update resources using cmdlets or commands like **Set-AZ Resource** or **AZ resource update**, and delete resources using **Remove-AZ Resource** or **AZ resource delete**.

2.2.9 What is Azure Cloud Shell, and how does it relate to Azure PowerShell and Azure CLI?

Azure Cloud Shell is an integrated command-line environment within the Azure Portal. It provides access to both Azure PowerShell and Azure CLI, allowing users to run commands and scripts directly from their web browsers.

2.2.10 What are some best practices for secure scripting and automation with Azure PowerShell and Azure CLI?

Best practices include using service principals for automation, securing secrets using Azure Key Vault, regularly rotating credentials, and following security guidelines provided by Azure. Additionally, always ensure that scripts are written securely and adhere to Azure security policies.

2.3 Azure Resource Manager

2.3.1 What is Azure Resource Manager (ARM), and what role does it play in managing Azure resources?

Azure Resource Manager (ARM) is the management layer in Azure that provides a unified way to create, deploy, manage, and organize Azure resources. It simplifies resource management by allowing users to define and manage resources as a group, known as a resource group.

2.3.2 What is a Resource Group in Azure, and why is it important when working with ARM?

A Resource Group is a logical container for Azure resources that share a common lifecycle. It helps users manage, organize, and apply policies to a set of related resources. When working with ARM, resource groups are crucial for grouping and organizing resources for easier management.

2.3.3 How does Azure Resource Manager help with resource deployment and lifecycle management?

ARM uses templates, known as Azure Resource Manager templates or ARM templates, to define the desired state of resources in JSON format. Users can deploy resources consistently by specifying their configuration in these templates. ARM also supports updating, deleting, and scaling resources as needed, ensuring resource lifecycle management.

2.3.4 What is the role of role-based access control (RBAC) in Azure Resource Manager, and how does it enhance security and governance?

RBAC is a crucial feature in ARM that controls who can access and manage Azure resources. It allows administrators to assign specific roles and permissions to users and groups, ensuring that only authorized individuals can perform certain actions. This enhances security and governance by enforcing access controls and minimizing the risk of unauthorized changes.

2.3.5 Can you explain the concept of resource tagging in Azure Resource Manager and how it aids in resource organization and cost management?

Resource tagging in ARM involves applying metadata, such as labels or keywords, to Azure resources. It helps users categorize and organize resources based on attributes like cost center, environment, or purpose. Tags are valuable for cost allocation, tracking, and management, as they enable users to identify and report on resource usage more effectively.

2.3.6 What is the concept of resource tagging, and how does it help with resource management and tracking in Azure?

Resource tagging involves applying metadata to resources using name-value pairs. It helps in categorizing and tracking resources for billing, cost analysis, and management purposes within ARM.

2.3.7 Can you explain the concept of resource locks in Azure Resource Manager and when they should be used?

Resource locks are used to prevent accidental deletion or modification of critical Azure resources. They can be set at the resource group or individual resource level to protect against unwanted changes.

2.3.8 How does Azure Resource Manager support resource deployment in multiple Azure regions and across different subscriptions?

ARM templates can specify the target region and subscription for resource deployment. This flexibility allows resources to be deployed and managed across multiple regions and subscriptions using the same template.

2.3.9 What are some best practices for organizing and managing resources efficiently with Azure Resource Manager?

Best practices include using naming conventions for resources and resource groups, grouping related resources in the same resource group, applying resource tagging, using RBAC for access control, and using Azure Policy for compliance and governance.

ONLINE RESOURCES

Practice Paper

Link : https://forms.gle/gsd8CB34kCmUypjf7

QR Code :

Video Content

Link : https://www.youtube.com/playlist?list=PLzlh_31VWEFp3ynwA_kQilFAm8C5bzlue

QR Code :

Chapter 3: Azure Core Services

3.1 Virtual Machines and Virtual Networks

3.1.1 What is an Azure Virtual Machine (VM), and what are some common use cases for deploying VMs in Azure?

An Azure VM is a scalable and customizable computing resource that runs an operating system. Common use cases include hosting web applications, databases, development and testing environments, and running Windows or Linux workloads in the cloud.

3.1.2 How can users ensure high availability for Azure Virtual Machines, and what role do Availability Sets play in achieving this?

High availability for VMs can be ensured by placing them in Availability Sets. An Availability Set distributes VMs across multiple fault domains and update domains, ensuring that if one VM or domain fails, others remain available. This minimizes downtime and enhances reliability.

3.1.3 What is an Azure Virtual Network (VNet), and why is it essential when deploying resources in Azure?

An Azure Virtual Network (VNet) is a private network within Azure that allows users to securely connect Azure resources. It provides isolation, segmentation, and control over network traffic. VNets are essential for connecting VMs, services, and resources while maintaining network security and routing control.

3.1.4 What are Network Security Groups (NSGs) in Azure, and how do they contribute to network security within Virtual Networks?

Network Security Groups (NSGs) are Azure resources that act as virtual firewalls for controlling inbound and outbound network traffic to and from Azure resources. They help enforce network security by defining rules that permit or deny traffic based on source, destination, port, and protocol, enhancing the security posture of VMs and VNets.

3.1.5 Can you explain the concept of Azure Virtual Network Peering and its significance in connecting Virtual Networks?

Azure Virtual Network Peering allows VNets to communicate with each other securely, regardless of their geographical location or subscription. It enables resource sharing, cross-region redundancy, and collaboration between different VNets while maintaining isolation. Peering simplifies network architecture and enhances connectivity across Azure environments.

3.1.6 How can you scale Azure Virtual Machines to handle increased workloads, and what are the scaling options available?

VM scaling can be achieved through manual scaling, auto-scaling, or using Azure Virtual Machine Scale Sets. Auto-scaling adjusts the number of VM instances based on predefined criteria like CPU usage, ensuring optimal resource utilization.

3.1.7 What is Azure Site Recovery, and how does it help in disaster recovery and business continuity planning for VMs?

Azure Site Recovery is a service that replicates VMs to a secondary Azure region. In case of a disaster, VMs can be quickly failed over to the secondary region, ensuring business continuity.

3.1.8 Can you explain the concept of Azure Virtual Network Peering and its benefits for connecting multiple virtual networks?

Virtual Network Peering allows the seamless connection of virtual networks within the same Azure region or across regions. It facilitates communication between resources in different networks while keeping traffic within the Azure backbone network.

3.1.9 What is Azure ExpressRoute, and how does it provide private, dedicated connectivity to Azure services?

Azure ExpressRoute offers a dedicated, private connection from an on-premises data center to Azure services. It bypasses the public internet, providing higher security, lower latency, and more reliable network connectivity.

3.1.10 What are some best practices for optimizing VM and virtual network performance and cost efficiency in Azure?

Best practices include choosing the appropriate VM size, utilizing reserved instances for cost savings, optimizing network traffic, implementing NSGs and firewalls, and regularly monitoring and scaling resources based on demand.

3.2 Deploying Virtual Machines

3.2.1 What is an Azure Virtual Machine (VM), and what are some common use cases for deploying VMs in Azure?

An Azure VM is a scalable and customizable computing resource that runs an operating system. Common use cases include hosting web applications, databases, development and testing environments, and running Windows or Linux workloads in the cloud.

3.2.2 How can users ensure high availability for Azure Virtual Machines, and what role do Availability Sets play in achieving this?

High availability for VMs can be ensured by placing them in Availability Sets. An Availability Set distributes VMs across multiple fault domains and update domains, ensuring that if one VM or domain fails, others remain available. This minimizes downtime and enhances reliability.

3.2.3 What is an Azure Virtual Network (VNet), and why is it essential when deploying resources in Azure?

An Azure Virtual Network (VNet) is a private network within Azure that allows users to securely connect Azure resources. It provides isolation, segmentation, and control over network traffic. VNets are essential for connecting VMs, services, and resources while maintaining network security and routing control.

3.2.4 What are Network Security Groups (NSGs) in Azure, and how do they contribute to network security within Virtual Networks?

Network Security Groups (NSGs) are Azure resources that act as virtual firewalls for controlling inbound and outbound network traffic to and from Azure resources. They help enforce network security by defining rules that permit or deny traffic based on source, destination, port, and protocol, enhancing the security posture of VMs and VNets.

3.2.5 Can you explain the concept of Azure Virtual Network Peering and its significance in connecting Virtual Networks?

Azure Virtual Network Peering allows VNets to communicate with each other securely, regardless of their geographical location or subscription. It enables resource sharing, cross-region redundancy, and collaboration between different VNets while maintaining isolation. Peering simplifies network architecture and enhances connectivity across Azure environments.

3.2.6 What is Azure Availability Zones, and how can they enhance the resilience and high availability of VM deployments?

Azure Availability Zones are data center locations within an Azure region with independent power, cooling, and networking. Deploying VMs across availability zones ensures redundancy and high availability in case of failures.

3.2.7 Can you explain the concept of Azure Virtual Machine images and how they simplify VM provisioning?

Azure VM images are snapshots of VMs that capture the VM's state, including the OS, software, and data. These images can be used to create new VMs with identical configurations, simplifying provisioning and replication.

3.2.8 How do you customize and configure a VM after it's deployed in Azure?

VM customization can be done by connecting to the VM via SSH or RDP. You can install software, configure settings, and apply updates as needed to meet specific requirements.

3.2.9 What is the role of Azure Resource Manager (ARM) in managing the lifecycle of Virtual Machines, including deployment, updates, and deletion?

ARM simplifies VM management by enabling users to define resource configurations and apply them consistently across deployments. It manages the entire VM lifecycle, from creation to updates and deletions.

3.3 Managing Virtual Networks

3.3.1 What is Azure Virtual Network (VNet) peering, and why is it important in managing VNets?

Azure VNet peering allows the connection of two VNets, enabling seamless communication between resources in different VNets. It's important for network segmentation, resource isolation, and simplifying network architecture without compromising security.

3.3.2 How can you secure traffic within a Virtual Network in Azure, and what role do Network Security Groups (NSGs) play?

To secure traffic, you can use Network Security Groups (NSGs) to define rules that control inbound and outbound traffic based on source, destination, port, and protocol. NSGs act as virtual firewalls, enhancing network security within the VNet.

3.3.3 What are Azure ExpressRoute and VPN Gateway, and how do they provide connectivity options for VNets?

Azure ExpressRoute is a private, dedicated connection to Azure from on-premises data centers, providing a high-speed and reliable link. VPN Gateway, on the other hand, offers secure site-to-site and remote access connectivity over the public internet. Both options extend on-premises networks to Azure VNets.

3.3.4 Can you explain the concept of Azure Virtual WAN and its role in managing multiple VNets?

Azure Virtual WAN is a networking service that simplifies and optimizes branch-to-branch and branch-to-Azure connectivity. It centralizes network management, including multiple VNets, hubs, and branches, making it easier to manage and optimize complex network architectures.

3.3.5 What is Azure Traffic Manager, and how can it be used to improve the availability and performance of applications across VNets?

Azure Traffic Manager is a DNS-based load balancer that directs incoming traffic to the most appropriate endpoint based on routing rules and health probes. It can distribute traffic across VNets and regions, improving application availability, scalability, and performance.

3.3.6 What role does Azure ExpressRoute play in Azure Virtual Networks, and how does it provide dedicated and private network connections?

Azure ExpressRoute offers private and dedicated connections to Azure data centers, bypassing the public internet. It ensures high-speed, low-latency, and secure network connectivity for Azure VNets.

3.3.7 How do you configure and manage DNS settings within an Azure Virtual Network for name resolution?

Azure VNets use Azure-provided DNS servers by default. Users can configure custom DNS settings for VNets to resolve names for resources within the VNet.

3.3.8 What are User-Defined Routes (UDR) in Azure VNets, and how do they allow users to control and customize network traffic routing?

User-Defined Routes (UDRs) enable users to specify custom routing paths for network traffic within a VNet. They are used to control traffic flow between subnets or to route traffic through specific network appliances.

3.3.9 What are some best practices for optimizing and securing Azure Virtual Networks, especially in large-scale deployments?

Best practices include segmenting VNets for isolation, implementing NSGs to control traffic, monitoring network performance, using ExpressRoute for dedicated connectivity, and regularly reviewing and updating network configurations for security and performance improvements.

3.4 Azure Availability Zones

3.4.1 What are Azure Availability Zones, and how do they contribute to high availability in Azure?

Azure Availability Zones are physically separate datacenter locations within an Azure region. They provide fault tolerance by ensuring that services and resources are redundantly deployed across zones. If one zone experiences an outage, services automatically failover to another zone, ensuring high availability.

3.4.2 How does Azure Availability Zones differ from Azure Availability Sets, and when should each be used?

Azure Availability Zones offer higher availability by distributing resources across multiple datacenter buildings, whereas Availability Sets distribute resources within a datacenter. Use Availability Zones for mission-critical workloads requiring the highest level of resilience and Availability Sets for less critical applications needing redundancy but not across zones.

3.4.3 Can you explain the concept of Azure Zone-redundant Virtual Machines, and why might organizations opt for this deployment model?

Zone-redundant Virtual Machines are VMs deployed across multiple Availability Zones. This provides even higher availability than single-zone VMs. Organizations choose this deployment model for business-critical applications that require continuous operation and minimal downtime.

3.4.4 How does Azure ensure that resources in different Availability Zones remain synchronized, and what technologies are used for this purpose?

Azure uses synchronous replication and redundant networking to ensure resources in different Availability Zones remain synchronized. Technologies like Azure Load Balancer and Azure Traffic Manager help route traffic and maintain consistency across zones.

3.4.5 What is the significance of the Service Level Agreement (SLA) associated with Azure Availability Zones, and what level of uptime does it guarantee?

The SLA for Azure Availability Zones guarantees 99.99% uptime for VMs and 99.95% uptime for Azure SQL Database. This means that Azure ensures highly reliable and available services within Availability Zones, minimizing unplanned downtime for critical workloads.

3.4.6 What happens in the event of a failure or outage in one Azure Availability Zone, and how does Azure handle failover?

In the event of a zone failure, resources in other Availability Zones remain unaffected, ensuring continuous availability. Azure automatically fails over resources to healthy zones to minimize downtime.

3.4.7 How can you ensure that your application or workload is designed for resilience across Azure Availability Zones?

Designing for resilience involves deploying resources across multiple Availability Zones, replicating data, and using load balancers and traffic management to distribute traffic across zones.

3.4.8 What is the Service Level Agreement (SLA) for Azure Availability Zones, and how does it guarantee uptime?

Azure Availability Zones offer a 99.99% SLA, ensuring that resources deployed in multiple zones will have minimal downtime and high availability.

3.4.9 Are Azure Availability Zones available in all Azure regions, and how can you determine if they are available in a specific region?

Availability Zones are not available in all Azure regions. You can check the Azure documentation to see the list of regions where Availability Zones are available.

3.4.10 What are some best practices for optimizing resource deployment and cost management in Azure Availability Zones?

Best practices include evaluating the need for zone redundancy, using zone-redundant services when necessary, regularly monitoring resource health, and considering cost implications when deploying resources in multiple zones.

ONLINE RESOURCES

Practice Paper

Link : https://forms.gle/XVpv6J6X9ACPpytA6

QR Code :

Video Content

Link :

https://www.youtube.com/playlist?list=PLzlh_31VWEFqWLxex3SQBEaVlhIJM74xi

QR Code :

Chapter 4: Azure Storage Services

4.1 Azure Blob Storage

4.1.1 What is Azure Blob Storage, and how does it differ from other types of storage services in Azure?

Azure Blob Storage is a scalable and cost-effective object storage service that stores unstructured data like documents, images, videos, and backups. It differs from other Azure storage options by specializing in large, unstructured data while offering features like hierarchical namespace and tiered storage.

4.1.2 What are the different access tiers available in Azure Blob Storage, and when should each be used?

Azure Blob Storage offers three access tiers: Hot, Cool, and Archive. Use the Hot tier for frequently accessed data, Cool for infrequently accessed data with lower storage costs, and Archive for data with long-term retention and the lowest costs but with retrieval delays.

4.1.3 How can you secure data stored in Azure Blob Storage, and what are some security features available?

Data in Azure Blob Storage can be secured using Azure Active Directory (Azure AD) authentication, Shared Access Signatures (SAS), and role-based access control (RBAC). Additionally, encryption at rest and in transit ensures data security.

4.1.4 What is the purpose of the Azure Blob Storage hierarchical namespace, and how does it simplify data organization?

The hierarchical namespace in Azure Blob Storage enables data organization using a folder-like structure within containers. It simplifies data management by providing a logical organization, making it easier to manage and navigate large datasets.

4.1.5 How does Azure Blob Storage support data replication and disaster recovery, and what are the redundancy options available?

Azure Blob Storage offers data replication across multiple Azure datacenters, providing redundancy and disaster recovery capabilities. The available replication options include Locally Redundant Storage (LRS), Geo-Redundant Storage (GRS), and Zone-Redundant Storage (ZRS), each offering different levels of data durability and availability.

4.1.6 What is Azure Blob Storage's integration with Azure Data Lake Storage, and how does it enable data analytics and processing?

Azure Blob Storage is integrated with Azure Data Lake Storage Gen2, allowing you to analyze and process data using Azure Data Lake Analytics, Azure Databricks, and other big data services.

4.1.7 What are some use cases for Azure Blob Storage, and can you provide examples of industries or scenarios that benefit from it?

Azure Blob Storage is used for backup and restore, media streaming, data archiving, content delivery, IoT data storage, and more. Industries like healthcare, media, and finance benefit from its versatility.

4.1.8 How can you optimize the performance of data access to Azure Blob Storage, especially for large datasets?

Optimizing performance involves choosing the appropriate storage tier (e.g., Hot, Cool, Archive), leveraging Azure CDN for content delivery, using parallelism in data transfers, and minimizing data access latency.

4.1.9 What is the difference between Azure Blob Storage and Azure Files, and when would you choose one over the other?

Azure Blob Storage is optimized for object storage, while Azure Files is a managed file share service. Choose Blob Storage for unstructured data like images and files, and Azure Files for file-based applications and shared file storage.

4.2 Azure Table Storage

4.2.1 What is Azure Table Storage, and how does it differ from other Azure storage services like Azure Blob Storage or Azure SQL Database?

Azure Table Storage is a NoSQL data store that allows you to store structured data in a key/attribute format. Unlike Azure Blob Storage, which stores unstructured data, or Azure SQL Database, which stores relational data, Azure Table Storage is designed for semi-structured and schema-less data.

4.2.2 How can you create and manage tables in Azure Table Storage, and what are some common use cases for this service?

Tables in Azure Table Storage are created programmatically using the Azure SDK or REST API. Common use cases include storing large volumes of structured data, logging, IoT telemetry data, and building scalable web applications with a schema-less design.

4.2.3 What is a Partition Key and Row Key in Azure Table Storage, and why are they essential for data retrieval?

The Partition Key and Row Key are two primary attributes in an Azure Table Storage entity. The Partition Key determines the partition where the data is stored, while the Row Key uniquely identifies the record within that partition. They are essential for efficient data retrieval and querying.

4.2.4 How does Azure Table Storage handle data consistency, and what consistency models are available for read operations?

Azure Table Storage provides two consistency models for read operations: Strong and Eventual. Strong consistency ensures that a read operation returns the most recent committed data, while eventual consistency allows for lower latency but may return slightly outdated data.

4.2.5 What are some best practices for optimizing performance and managing costs when using Azure Table Storage?

Best practices include designing efficient data models, optimizing queries using appropriate partition and row keys, using batch operations to minimize request costs, and considering data retention and archival strategies to control costs over time. Properly designing your data model is crucial for achieving the best performance and cost-efficiency in Table Storage.

4.2.6 What is the role of secondary indexes in Azure Table Storage, and how do they impact query performance?

Secondary indexes in Azure Table Storage allow users to perform efficient range queries and filters on non-key attributes. They improve query performance but require additional storage and maintenance.

4.2.7 How can you secure data in Azure Table Storage, and what authentication and authorization mechanisms are available?

Data in Azure Table Storage can be secured using Shared Access Signatures (SAS) tokens, Azure RBAC, and Azure AD authentication. SAS tokens provide granular control over data access.

4.2.8 What are some common use cases for Azure Table Storage, and can you provide examples of scenarios where it is particularly useful?

Azure Table Storage is commonly used for logging, IoT telemetry data, user session management, and storing semi-structured data that doesn't require complex querying.

4.2.9 What is the recommended approach for designing and modeling data in Azure Table Storage, especially when dealing with evolving data schemas?
Design data models in Azure Table Storage to be flexible and accommodate evolving schemas. Avoid nested structures and plan for efficient querying based on access patterns and queries.

4.3 Azure File Storage

4.3.1 What is Azure File Storage, and how does it differ from Azure Blob Storage and Azure Disk Storage?
Azure File Storage is a fully managed file share service in the cloud, offering SMB and NFS file-sharing protocols. Unlike Azure Blob Storage, it's designed for structured data and supports file-level operations. In contrast to Azure Disk Storage, it provides a shared file system accessible by multiple VMs.

4.3.2 How can you mount Azure File Shares to on-premises servers, and what use cases are suitable for hybrid cloud scenarios?
Azure File Shares can be mounted to on-premises servers using Azure File Sync, a service that enables synchronization between on-premises file servers and Azure File Shares. This is valuable for hybrid cloud scenarios where organizations need to centralize file storage, enable remote access, and maintain data consistency.

4.3.3 What is the difference between Azure Files Standard and Premium tiers, and when should each be chosen?
Azure Files Standard is designed for general-purpose file sharing and offers cost-effective storage. Azure Files Premium provides higher performance and low-latency access for workloads with demanding I/O requirements. Choose the tier that aligns with your application's performance needs and budget.

4.3.4 How does Azure File Storage ensure data durability and high availability, and what replication options are available?
Azure File Storage ensures data durability by replicating data within an Azure region. The available replication options include Locally Redundant Storage (LRS), Geo-Redundant Storage (GRS), and Zone-Redundant Storage (ZRS). Each option offers different levels of redundancy and availability.

4.3.5 Can you explain how Azure File Storage integrates with Azure Active Directory (Azure AD) for authentication and authorization?
Azure File Storage supports Azure AD authentication, allowing you to control access to file shares using Azure AD identities. This simplifies identity management and enhances security by ensuring that only authorized users and applications can access Azure File Shares.

4.3.6 How can you monitor and optimize the performance of Azure File Storage, especially for applications with high I/O requirements?
Performance can be optimized by choosing the appropriate SKU (Standard or Premium), monitoring throughput and latency metrics, enabling Azure File Sync for caching, and distributing load across multiple file shares or directories.

4.3.7 What are the durability and availability guarantees provided by Azure File Storage, and how does it ensure data resilience?
Azure File Storage offers high durability with redundant storage and multiple replicas of data. It also benefits from Azure's built-in data replication and backup capabilities, ensuring data resilience.

4.3.8 How does Azure File Storage integrate with Azure Backup and Azure Site Recovery for data protection and disaster recovery?

Azure File Storage can be backed up using Azure Backup, providing point-in-time recovery. It can also be integrated with Azure Site Recovery for disaster recovery scenarios, ensuring business continuity.

4.3.9 What are some best practices for optimizing cost and performance when using Azure File Storage, especially in large-scale deployments?

Best practices include using Premium File Shares for high I/O workloads, optimizing data layout, monitoring storage metrics, and using tiering to lower costs for less frequently accessed data.

4.3.10 How can you migrate existing on-premises file shares to Azure File Storage, and what tools or services are available for this purpose?

Azure File Sync and Azure Data Box are two common options for migrating existing on-premises file shares to Azure File Storage. Azure Data Factory can also be used for large-scale data transfers.

ONLINE RESOURCES

Practice Paper

Link : https://forms.gle/YYBzrEn6cBKthgd1A

QR Code :

Video Content

Link : https://www.youtube.com/playlist?list=PLzlh_31VWEFqYT2WoU09aJZ-dhNYmFtUr

QR Code :

Chapter 5: Azure Identity and Access Management

5.1 Azure Active Directory

5.1.1 What is Azure Active Directory, and how does it differ from on-premises Active Directory?

Azure Active Directory is a cloud-based identity and access management service provided by Microsoft. While on-premises Active Directory is used for managing identities within a corporate network, Azure AD extends identity management to cloud-based applications and services, allowing users to authenticate from anywhere.

5.1.2 What are the primary roles and functions of Azure AD, and how does it contribute to security in Azure?

Azure AD serves as an identity provider and offers features such as user authentication, Single Sign-On (SSO), Multi-Factor Authentication (MFA), and identity governance. It plays a crucial role in enhancing security by controlling access to Azure resources and applications.

5.1.3 What is Azure AD B2B (Business-to-Business), and how can organizations use it to collaborate with external partners?

Azure AD B2B allows organizations to collaborate securely with external partners by inviting them to use their own Azure AD or social identities for authentication. This enables controlled access to resources without the need for separate accounts.

5.1.4What is Azure AD Connect, and how does it synchronize on-premises Active Directory with Azure AD?

Azure AD Connect is a tool used to synchronize on-premises Active Directory with Azure AD. It ensures that user accounts, groups, and attributes are kept consistent between the on-premises environment and the Azure cloud, enabling seamless authentication and identity management.

5.1.5 How does Azure AD support role-based access control (RBAC), and what are some best practices for implementing RBAC in Azure?

Azure AD integrates with Azure RBAC to assign roles and permissions to users and groups. Best practices for RBAC include role segregation, assigning the least privilege necessary, regularly reviewing access, and using built-in roles whenever possible to simplify access management.

5.1.6 How can you integrate Azure AD with other SaaS applications and services, and what protocols does it support for single sign-on (SSO)?

Azure AD supports integration with thousands of SaaS applications using protocols like SAML, OAuth, and OpenID Connect for SSO. Azure AD Application Proxy allows secure access to on-premises web apps.

5.1.7 What is Azure AD Domain Services, and how does it extend on-premises Active Directory capabilities to Azure VMs without the need for a VPN?

Azure AD Domain Services provides domain controller functionality in Azure. It enables authentication and domain-join capabilities for Azure VMs without requiring a VPN connection to on-premises AD.

5.1.8 How does Azure AD protect against identity-based attacks like password spray attacks and brute force attacks?

Azure AD uses risk-based adaptive authentication and smart lockout policies to detect and respond to identity-based attacks, helping to protect against unauthorized access.

5.1.9 What are Azure AD Identity Protection and Azure AD Privileged Identity Management (PIM), and how do they enhance security for Azure AD?

Azure AD Identity Protection identifies and responds to risky sign-in attempts, while Azure AD PIM manages, monitors, and audits privileged roles, reducing the risk of privilege misuse.

5.2 Role-Based Access Control (RBAC)

5.2.1 What is Role-Based Access Control (RBAC), and why is it important in cloud computing and Azure?

RBAC is a security model that defines and manages access permissions based on roles and their associated privileges. In cloud computing and Azure, RBAC is crucial for ensuring that users and services have appropriate and limited access to resources, helping organizations maintain security and compliance.

5.2.2 How does RBAC work in Azure, and what are the core components of RBAC roles?

RBAC in Azure assigns roles to Azure resources, subscriptions, and management groups. Core components of RBAC roles include Role Definitions (defining permissions), Role Assignments (associating roles with users or groups), and the Azure AD (Azure Active Directory) for user and group management.

5.2.3 What is the principle of least privilege, and how does it relate to RBAC best practices?

The principle of least privilege is a security concept that advises granting users or processes the minimum level of access required to perform their tasks. In RBAC, applying this principle ensures that users have only the necessary permissions to carry out their responsibilities, reducing the risk of unauthorized access and potential breaches.

5.2.4 How can you create custom RBAC roles in Azure, and when might organizations need to define custom roles?

Organizations can create custom RBAC roles in Azure by modifying existing built-in roles or defining new ones with specific permissions. Custom roles are often needed when built-in roles do not precisely match the organization's access requirements or when granular control is necessary.

5.2.5 What are some common RBAC best practices for managing access to Azure resources effectively and securely?

RBAC best practices include:

- Regularly reviewing and auditing role assignments.
- Avoiding the use of overly permissive roles.
- Assigning roles to Azure AD groups for easier management.
- Restricting the assignment of owner roles to prevent excessive access.
- Implementing a role naming convention for consistency and clarity.

5.2.6 What is "just-in-time" (JIT) access in Azure RBAC, and how does it enhance security for privileged roles?

JIT access allows users to request temporary access to privileged roles for a specific time window. It reduces the exposure of privileged roles and requires approval for access.

5.2.7 Can you describe the concept of "deny" assignments in Azure RBAC and how they can be used to restrict access even further?

"Deny" assignments are used to explicitly deny certain permissions to users or groups, even if they have been granted those permissions through role assignments. They are useful for implementing stricter access controls.

5.2.7 How does RBAC integrate with Azure Policy, and what role do initiatives and assignments play in governing Azure resources?

RBAC and Azure Policy work together to enforce governance policies. Initiatives define sets of policies, and assignments apply those policies to specific scopes (e.g., subscriptions or resource groups) based on RBAC roles.

5.2.8 What is the role of Azure Blueprints in RBAC, and how do they help ensure compliance and consistency in resource deployments?

Azure Blueprints provide a way to define and enforce standardized configurations for Azure environments, including RBAC roles, policies, and resource groups, ensuring compliance with organizational standards.

5.2.9 What are some best practices for effectively managing RBAC in large-scale Azure environments and ensuring least privilege access?

Best practices include using built-in roles whenever possible, regularly reviewing and auditing role assignments, using Azure AD groups for role assignments, and implementing a strong naming convention for custom roles to enhance manageability.

5.3 Multi-Factor Authentication (MFA)

5.3.1 What is Multi-Factor Authentication (MFA), and why is it considered an important security measure?

MFA is a security method that requires users to provide two or more authentication factors to access an account or system. It enhances security by adding an extra layer of verification beyond just a password, making it significantly more challenging for unauthorized users to gain access.

5.3.2 What are the common authentication factors used in MFA, and how do they contribute to enhanced security?

Common authentication factors include something you know (password or PIN), something you have (a smartphone, smart card, or hardware token), and something you are (biometric data like fingerprints or facial recognition). These factors collectively increase security by requiring multiple forms of verification.

5.3.3 How can organizations implement MFA in their environments, and what are the benefits of integrating MFA with Azure Active Directory (Azure AD)?

Organizations can implement MFA by integrating it with identity providers like Azure AD. Benefits include improved security, reduced risk of unauthorized access, compliance with regulatory requirements, and protection against phishing and credential theft.

5.3.4 What are some common challenges or considerations when implementing MFA, and how can organizations address them?

Challenges include user adoption and convenience, device compatibility, and managing MFA policies at scale. Organizations can address these challenges by providing user training, offering user-friendly MFA methods, and using identity and access management tools to streamline policy enforcement.

5.3.5 Can you explain the concept of adaptive MFA, and how does it enhance security while maintaining user experience?

Adaptive MFA is an intelligent approach that evaluates risk factors and adapts MFA requirements accordingly. It can increase authentication requirements when suspicious activity is detected while reducing friction for trusted users. This enhances security without compromising the user experience.

5.3.6 How can organizations balance security with user convenience when implementing Azure MFA, and what are some user-friendly authentication methods available?

Organizations can balance security and convenience by offering user-friendly authentication methods like biometric recognition, push notifications, and time-based one-time passwords (TOTP) in addition to traditional methods.

5.3.7 What are some common use cases for Azure MFA in Azure environments, and how does it address specific security challenges?

Common use cases include securing remote access to Azure resources, protecting privileged accounts, and ensuring secure access to sensitive data. Azure MFA addresses these use cases by adding an extra layer of security.

5.3.8 How does Azure MFA integrate with Azure Active Directory, and what role does Azure AD play in managing user access and authentication?

Azure MFA integrates seamlessly with Azure AD, allowing administrators to enable MFA for specific users or groups. Azure AD serves as the identity and access management hub for Azure resources.

5.3.9 What are some best practices for configuring and managing Azure MFA to ensure smooth operations and effective security?

Best practices include defining clear policies, regularly reviewing MFA reports and logs, testing MFA configurations, and educating users about the importance of MFA.

ONLINE RESOURCES

Practice Paper

Link : https://forms.gle/TLhrGzbMsMcX6P118

QR Code :

Video Content

Link :

https://www.youtube.com/playlist?list=PLzlh_31VWEFpFG3cjp6UwEkbUdTpT2w4e

QR Code :

Chapter 6: Azure Solutions

6.1 Azure App Services

6.1.1 What is Azure App Service, and what types of applications can be hosted on it?
Azure App Service is a fully managed platform for building, deploying, and scaling web apps and APIs. It supports a wide range of applications, including web applications, mobile app backends, RESTful APIs, and serverless functions.

6.1.2 What is the key difference between Azure Web Apps and Azure Functions, and when should each be used?
Azure Web Apps are used for hosting web applications with structured frameworks, while Azure Functions are used for serverless, event-driven, and granular code execution. Choose Web Apps for traditional web applications and Functions for event-driven, serverless workloads.

6.1.3 How does Azure App Service provide scalability and high availability for hosted applications, and what are deployment slots?
Azure App Service offers automatic scaling based on demand and geographic distribution for high availability. Deployment slots are separate environments for testing and staging apps, allowing seamless code deployment and rollback without impacting the production environment.

6.1.4 Can you explain the concept of Azure App Service plans, and how do they affect the performance and cost of hosted applications?
App Service plans determine the region, capacity, and features for the hosted applications. They affect performance and cost by specifying the resources available, including CPU, memory, and scalability options. Different plans cater to various application requirements and budget constraints.

6.1.5 What are the options for deploying applications to Azure App Service, and how does continuous integration (CI/CD) play a role in the deployment process?
Applications can be deployed to Azure App Service using various methods, including Azure DevOps, GitHub Actions, Visual Studio, and Azure CLI. CI/CD pipelines automate the deployment process, ensuring that changes are tested, validated, and deployed efficiently, reducing manual errors and deployment time.

6.1.6 Can you explain the integration of Azure App Services with Azure DevOps for continuous integration and continuous deployment (CI/CD)?
Azure App Services integrate seamlessly with Azure DevOps, enabling automated CI/CD pipelines. Developers can automate code deployments, testing, and monitoring for their web apps.

6.1.7 What is Azure Functions, and how does it differ from Azure App Services in terms of serverless application development?
Azure Functions is a serverless compute service, while Azure App Services provide a managed platform for web applications. Azure Functions are event-driven and can execute code in response to events, making them suitable for microservices and event-driven scenarios.

6.1.8 How does Azure App Service handle security and compliance for hosted web applications, and what security features are available?
Azure App Service provides features like Web Application Firewall (WAF), SSL/TLS encryption, authentication and authorization, and Azure AD integration to enhance application security and compliance.

6.1.9 What are the options for custom domain and SSL certificate management in Azure App Services, and how can you secure traffic to custom domains?

Azure App Services allow custom domain binding and support SSL certificates. You can bring your SSL certificates or use Azure's built-in certificate management to secure traffic to custom domains.

6.1.10 What are some common use cases and scenarios where Azure App Services are a suitable choice for hosting web applications, and can you provide examples?

Azure App Services are ideal for hosting web applications, APIs, and mobile backends. Common use cases include e-commerce sites, content management systems, IoT backends, and RESTful APIs for mobile apps.

6.2 Web Apps

6.2.1 What is a Web App, and how does it differ from traditional web hosting methods?

A Web App is a cloud-based service that allows developers to build, host, and scale web applications without managing infrastructure. It differs from traditional hosting as it abstracts away server management, offering automatic scaling, load balancing, and easy deployment.

6.2.2 What is the significance of platform as a service (PaaS) in the context of Web Apps, and how does it benefit developers?

Web Apps are a prime example of PaaS, where the platform handles underlying infrastructure concerns, such as OS maintenance and server provisioning. This allows developers to focus solely on coding, accelerating development and reducing operational overhead.

6.2.3 How can you configure custom domains and SSL certificates for Azure Web Apps, and why is this important for web applications?

Custom domains and SSL certificates can be configured in the Azure portal. This is crucial for branding, SEO, and security. SSL certificates encrypt data transmitted between the user's browser and the web app, enhancing data protection and user trust.

6.2.4 Can you explain the concept of deployment slots in Azure Web Apps, and how do they benefit the deployment process?

Deployment slots are separate instances of a web app used for staging and testing. They facilitate seamless deployment of changes while maintaining a production-like environment. Slots enable A/B testing, blue-green deployments, and rollback capabilities without impacting the live app.

6.2.5 What is Azure App Service Environment (ASE), and when might organizations consider using it for hosting their Web Apps?

Azure App Service Environment is a premium service plan for Web Apps that offers a fully isolated, highly scalable environment. Organizations might choose ASE for compliance requirements, high-level isolation, and the ability to run web apps in their own virtual network.

6.2.6 What are the security features provided by Azure Web Apps to protect web applications from common vulnerabilities and threats?

Azure Web Apps offer security features such as Web Application Firewall (WAF), SSL/TLS encryption, authentication and authorization settings, and integrated Azure AD authentication to protect against common web application threats.

6.2.7 Can you describe how custom domains and SSL certificates can be configured and managed for Azure Web Apps?

Azure Web Apps allow custom domains to be mapped, and SSL certificates can be uploaded or purchased through Azure. Options for securing traffic to custom domains include using Azure's built-in certificate management or bringing your SSL certificates.

6.2.8 What are the considerations when choosing between Linux-based and Windows-based Azure Web Apps for hosting web applications?

Consider the programming languages and frameworks your application uses. Windows-based Web Apps support ASP.NET, while Linux-based Web Apps are suitable for applications using technologies like Node.js, PHP, and Python.

6.2.9 How does Azure Web Apps integrate with Azure Monitor and Application Insights to provide performance monitoring and diagnostics for web applications?

Azure Web Apps integrate with Azure Monitor and Application Insights to provide real-time performance monitoring, logging, and diagnostics. These tools help identify and troubleshoot issues in web applications.

6.2.10 What are some common use cases for Azure Web Apps, and can you provide examples of scenarios where they are particularly useful?

Azure Web Apps are ideal for hosting websites, web APIs, and web applications. Common use cases include e-commerce websites, content management systems (CMS), blogging platforms, and RESTful APIs for mobile apps.

6.3 API Apps

6.3.1 What is an API App, and how does it differ from traditional APIs?

An API App is a specific type of Azure Web App designed for hosting APIs. It provides a scalable and managed platform for building, deploying, and securing APIs. Unlike traditional APIs, API Apps are hosted in the Azure App Service environment, offering robust scaling and management features.

6.3.2 How can API Apps be secured and authenticated, and what authentication methods does Azure API Management offer?

API Apps can be secured using Azure Active Directory (Azure AD), OAuth 2.0, or API keys. Azure API Management offers various authentication methods, including subscription keys, OAuth, and client certificates, to control access to API endpoints.

6.3.3 What are the benefits of using Azure API Management alongside API Apps, and how does it simplify API management and consumption?

Azure API Management acts as a gateway for API Apps, providing features like rate limiting, caching, analytics, and developer portal creation. It simplifies API management, documentation, and access control, making it easier for developers to consume and for organizations to manage APIs.

6.3.4 Can you explain the concept of API versioning in API Apps, and why is it important for maintaining backward compatibility?

API versioning allows multiple versions of an API to coexist, ensuring backward compatibility for existing clients while allowing new features to be introduced. It's important for ensuring that changes to the API do not break existing integrations.

6.3.5 How does Azure Logic Apps integrate with API Apps, and what scenarios can be achieved by combining these services?

Azure Logic Apps can connect to and trigger API Apps, allowing for workflow automation based on API events. This integration enables scenarios like data synchronization, notifications, and process automation when specific API actions occur.

6.3.6 How does Azure API Apps handle versioning of APIs, and what best practices should be followed to manage API versioning effectively?

Azure API Apps allow API versioning through URL paths or query parameters. Best practices include using semantic versioning, providing clear documentation, and maintaining backward compatibility.

6.3.7 What role does Azure Functions play in conjunction with API Apps, and how can they be used to create serverless APIs?
Azure Functions can be used with API Apps to create serverless APIs. Functions can execute code in response to HTTP requests, enabling serverless API endpoints for specific functions or microservices.
6.3.8 How can developers handle API authentication and authorization for third-party clients or mobile apps consuming API Apps?
API Apps support various authentication methods, including OAuth 2.0 and API keys. Developers can configure authentication and authorization mechanisms to grant access to third-party clients securely.
6.3.9 Can you provide examples of real-world scenarios where Azure API Apps are particularly useful, and describe how they solve specific business problems?
Azure API Apps are useful in scenarios like building a RESTful API for a mobile app, creating a backend API for a web application, or integrating with third-party services, such as payment gateways or social media platforms, to facilitate data exchange and streamline processes.

6.4 Azure Functions

6.4.1 What is Azure Functions, and how does it fit into the serverless computing paradigm?
Azure Functions is a serverless compute service that allows developers to run event-driven code without managing infrastructure. It enables automatic scaling, making it ideal for executing short-lived functions in response to various triggers.
6.4.2 What are the different types of triggers available for Azure Functions, and can you provide examples of when each trigger might be used?
Azure Functions supports various triggers, including HTTP triggers for webhooks, timer triggers for scheduled tasks, and event triggers for services like Azure Storage and Azure Service Bus. Each trigger type is used to respond to specific events or conditions.
6.4.3 How can you secure and authenticate Azure Functions, and what role does Azure Active Directory (Azure AD) play in this process?
Azure Functions can be secured using built-in authentication and authorization features, such as Function Keys, Managed Identity, and Azure AD authentication. Azure AD integration enables user and application-based authentication for added security.
6.4.4 What are Durable Functions in Azure, and how do they extend the capabilities of Azure Functions?
Durable Functions is an extension of Azure Functions that simplifies stateful and long-running workflows. It enables orchestrations, fan-out/fan-in patterns, and reliable messaging between functions, allowing developers to build complex, reliable, and scalable workflows.
6.4.5 How does Azure Functions pricing work, and what factors should organizations consider to optimize costs when using this serverless service?
Azure Functions pricing is based on resource consumption, execution time, and the number of executions. To optimize costs, organizations should consider function design, execution frequency, and appropriate scaling settings, ensuring resources are used efficiently and costs are minimized.
6.4.6 How can Azure Functions be secured to protect sensitive data and prevent unauthorized access?
Azure Functions can be secured using Azure Active Directory (Azure AD) authentication, API keys, and integration with Azure Key Vault for storing and managing secrets securely.

6.4.7 What role do Azure Logic Apps and Azure Event Grid play in conjunction with Azure Functions, and how do they enhance event-driven workflows?
Azure Logic Apps provide workflow automation, while Azure Event Grid facilitates event-driven architectures. Azure Functions can be triggered by events from both Logic Apps and Event Grid, enabling seamless integration and automation.
6.4.8 What are some best practices for monitoring and troubleshooting Azure Functions, and what tools and services can be used for this purpose?
Best practices include using Application Insights for monitoring, logging, and telemetry. Azure Monitor provides a centralized location for monitoring and diagnosing function apps.
6.4.9 Can you provide examples of real-world scenarios where Azure Functions are particularly useful, and describe how they solve specific business problems?
Azure Functions are useful for scenarios such as processing IoT device data, automating data workflows, handling real-time data stream processing, and creating serverless APIs for mobile and web applications. They streamline development and reduce operational overhead in these scenarios.

ONLINE RESOURCES

Practice Paper
Link : https://forms.gle/vRX6mThXJTBKrau87

QR Code :

Video Content
Link :
https://www.youtube.com/playlist?list=PLzlh_31VWEFqZUZRBOTSPqmFPJtRYpCkQ

QR Code :

Chapter 7: Azure Databases

7.1 Azure SQL Database

7.1.1 What is Azure SQL Database, and how does it differ from traditional SQL Server installations?

Azure SQL Database is a fully managed relational database service in the cloud. Unlike traditional SQL Server installations, it abstracts away infrastructure management tasks, such as patching and scaling, while offering high availability, security, and automatic backups.

7.1.2 What are the different deployment options for Azure SQL Database, and how do they cater to various workload requirements?

Azure SQL Database offers options such as Single Database, Elastic Pool, and Managed Instance. Single Database is suitable for individual databases, Elastic Pool is ideal for multi-tenant applications, and Managed Instance provides compatibility with on-premises SQL Server for lift-and-shift scenarios.

7.1.3 How can you ensure data security and compliance in Azure SQL Database, and what built-in features assist with this?

Azure SQL Database includes features like Transparent Data Encryption (TDE), Azure Active Directory authentication, Auditing, and Advanced Threat Protection. These features help secure data and assist organizations in meeting compliance requirements.

7.1.4 What is Azure SQL Database's automatic tuning, and how does it optimize database performance?

Azure SQL Database's automatic tuning uses machine learning to monitor and adjust database performance parameters, such as query optimization and index maintenance. It continuously improves performance without manual intervention, reducing query latency and resource utilization.

7.1.5 Can you explain the high availability and disaster recovery options available for Azure SQL Database, and how do they ensure business continuity?

Azure SQL Database offers options like geo-replication and automatic failover groups for high availability. Geo-replication replicates data to a secondary region for disaster recovery, ensuring data redundancy and minimizing downtime in case of region-wide outages. Automatic failover groups provide automatic failover between databases in different regions for seamless continuity.

7.1.6 How does Azure SQL Database handle automated backups and point-in-time restore, and what is the retention period for backups?

Azure SQL Database provides automated daily backups with a retention period of up to 35 days. You can perform point-in-time restores to recover data to a specific moment in time.

7.1.7 What are the benefits of using Azure Managed Instance over traditional Azure SQL Database deployments, and in what scenarios is it recommended?

Azure Managed Instance offers full SQL Server compatibility, allowing easy migration of on-premises databases. It's recommended for lift-and-shift migrations or scenarios where you need more control over the database engine.

7.1.8 How can you optimize the performance of Azure SQL Database, and what tools and features are available for monitoring and tuning performance?

Performance optimization involves query tuning, indexing, and utilizing features like Query Store. Azure Monitor and Query Performance Insights provide tools for monitoring and identifying performance issues.

7.1.9 What is Geo-Replication in Azure SQL Database, and how does it enable disaster recovery and business continuity?
Geo-Replication allows you to replicate databases to different regions for disaster recovery. It creates readable secondary databases that can also be used for load balancing read-heavy workloads.

7.2 Cosmos DB

7.2.1 What is Azure Cosmos DB, and how does it differ from traditional relational databases?
Azure Cosmos DB is a globally distributed, multi-model database service in the cloud. Unlike traditional relational databases, Cosmos DB is designed for horizontal scalability, low-latency access, and support for various data models, including document, key-value, graph, and column-family.

7.2.2 How does Cosmos DB achieve global distribution, and what are the benefits of multi-region replication?
Cosmos DB achieves global distribution through multi-region replication, allowing data to be synchronized across multiple Azure regions. Benefits include low-latency access for users worldwide, automatic failover, high availability, and data residency compliance.

7.2.3 What is the significance of Cosmos DB's multiple data models, and how can developers choose the most suitable model for their applications?
Cosmos DB's support for multiple data models enables developers to choose the most appropriate model for their application's data structure and access patterns. It accommodates diverse workloads, simplifying development and reducing the need for separate database services.

7.2.4 How does Cosmos DB ensure high availability and data consistency, and what consistency models are available?
Cosmos DB provides high availability through automatic replication and failover. It offers five consistency models: Strong, Bounded staleness, Session, Consistent Prefix, and Eventual, allowing developers to choose the level of consistency that best suits their application's requirements.

7.2.5 What are the pricing considerations for Cosmos DB, and how can organizations optimize costs while using this globally distributed database service?
Cosmos DB pricing is based on factors such as provisioned throughput, data storage, and regions. To optimize costs, organizations should carefully provision resources based on workload requirements, utilize auto-scaling, and consider data retention policies to manage storage costs effectively.

7.2.6 Can you explain the benefits of Azure Cosmos DB's automatic indexing, and how can developers optimize indexing for query performance?
Azure Cosmos DB automatically indexes data for efficient queries. Developers can optimize indexing by specifying custom indexing policies and using Composite Indexes for complex queries.

7.2.7 What are the security features provided by Azure Cosmos DB to protect data at rest and in transit, and how can encryption and authentication be configured?
Azure Cosmos DB encrypts data at rest and in transit using industry-standard encryption protocols. It supports Azure AD authentication, role-based access control (RBAC), and IP firewall rules for access control.

7.2.8 How can developers use Azure Functions and Azure Cosmos DB triggers to create serverless applications that react to database changes?

Azure Functions can be triggered by Cosmos DB changes, such as inserts or updates, to execute serverless code in response to data events, enabling real-time processing and event-driven applications.

7.2.9 What are the backup and recovery options available for Azure Cosmos DB, and how can data be restored in case of accidental data loss or corruption?

Azure Cosmos DB offers automatic and manual backups. You can use the Point-in-Time Restore feature to recover data to a specific timestamp in case of data loss or corruption.

7.2.10 Can you provide examples of real-world use cases where Azure Cosmos DB is particularly useful, and how does it address specific business needs?

Azure Cosmos DB is valuable for scenarios like IoT data storage, content management systems, real-time analytics, and globally distributed applications. It ensures low-latency data access, scalability, and high availability for these use cases.

7.3 Azure Database for MySQL and PostgreSQL

7.3.1 What is Azure Database for MySQL and PostgreSQL, and how do they differ from running MySQL and PostgreSQL databases on traditional servers?

Azure Database for MySQL and PostgreSQL are fully managed database services that offer the same database engines but abstract away infrastructure management. They provide automated backups, scaling, high availability, and security features, reducing operational overhead compared to self-hosted databases.

7.3.2 How can you migrate an existing on-premises MySQL or PostgreSQL database to Azure Database for MySQL or PostgreSQL, and what tools and methods are available?

Migration can be done using various tools like Azure Database Migration Service, Data Migration Assistant, or open-source utilities like pg_dump and mysqldump. The process involves exporting data from the source database, importing it into Azure, and modifying connection strings.

7.3.3 What are some key security features available in Azure Database for MySQL and PostgreSQL, and how can organizations protect their data in the cloud?

Both services offer features like Virtual Network Service Endpoints, SSL/TLS encryption, and Azure Active Directory authentication for securing data in transit and at rest. Additionally, firewall rules and auditing capabilities help control access and monitor database activity.

7.3.4 Can you explain the concept of automatic backups and point-in-time restore in Azure Database for MySQL and PostgreSQL?

Azure Database for MySQL and PostgreSQL automatically create backups of the database at regular intervals. Point-in-time restore allows users to recover their databases to specific points in time, helping to prevent data loss due to accidental changes or deletions.

7.3.5 How does Azure Database for MySQL and PostgreSQL ensure high availability, and what is the role of read replicas in improving database performance?

Azure Database for MySQL and PostgreSQL provide high availability through automatic failover and replication. Read replicas are secondary databases that can handle read-heavy workloads, offloading queries from the primary database and enhancing performance while maintaining data consistency.

7.3.6 Explain the automated backup and point-in-time restore capabilities of Azure Database for MySQL, and how can data be recovered in case of accidental deletion or data corruption?

Azure Database for MySQL provides automated daily backups with a retention period of up to 35 days. Point-in-time restore allows data recovery to a specific timestamp within the retention period.

7.3.7 What are some key performance optimization strategies for Azure Database for PostgreSQL, and how can indexing and query optimization be improved?

Performance optimization strategies include optimizing queries, using indexing effectively, and choosing an appropriate service tier based on resource requirements. Azure Monitor and Query Performance Insights can help identify performance bottlenecks.

7.3.8 How does Azure Database for PostgreSQL integrate with Azure Active Directory (Azure AD) for authentication and role-based access control (RBAC)?

Azure Database for PostgreSQL supports Azure AD integration, allowing users to authenticate using their Azure AD credentials. RBAC can be used to control access and permissions.

7.3.9 What is Azure Database for MySQL, and how does it provide a managed MySQL database service in the cloud?

Azure Database for MySQL is a fully managed relational database service that offers the MySQL database engine. It abstracts infrastructure management tasks, such as backups and patching, while providing high availability and scalability.Top of Form.

ONLINE RESOURCES

Practice Paper

Link : https://forms.gle/BPwr5ZNgfSQJqnNK6

QR Code :

Video Content

Link : https://www.youtube.com/playlist?list=PLzlh_31VWEFrZl4Oy6kj5xVpSregtDO09

QR Code :

Chapter 8: Azure Networking

8.1 Azure Virtual Network Gateway

8.1.1 What is an Azure Virtual Network Gateway, and what role does it play in Azure networking?

An Azure Virtual Network Gateway is a networking component that connects on-premises networks to Azure virtual networks. It serves as a VPN or ExpressRoute gateway, enabling secure communication between on-premises infrastructure and Azure resources.

8.1.2 What are the two main types of Azure Virtual Network Gateways, and when should you choose one over the other?

The two main types are VPN Gateway and ExpressRoute Gateway. VPN Gateway is used for secure connections over the public internet, while ExpressRoute Gateway is used for private, dedicated connections to Azure via an ExpressRoute circuit.

8.1.3 How does Azure Virtual Network Gateway ensure data encryption and secure communication between on-premises networks and Azure resources?

Azure Virtual Network Gateway uses industry-standard encryption protocols, such as IPsec and BGP, to secure data in transit. It also supports VPN tunneling and ExpressRoute for private, dedicated connectivity.

8.1.4 What is the purpose of Azure Virtual Network Gateway SKUs (Sizes), and how do they impact performance and scalability?

Virtual Network Gateway SKUs determine the gateway's performance, scalability, and features. Higher SKUs offer increased bandwidth, more tunnels, and additional features like BGP support. Organizations should choose a SKU that matches their specific networking requirements.

8.1.5 Can you explain the concept of active-active and active-passive configurations for Azure Virtual Network Gateways, and when might each be used?

Active-active configuration uses two gateways to load balance traffic for high availability and increased throughput. Active-passive configuration uses one primary and one secondary gateway for failover. Choose the appropriate configuration based on uptime and performance requirements.

8.1.6 What is the role of Border Gateway Protocol (BGP) in Azure Virtual Network Gateway, and how does it enable dynamic routing for VPN and ExpressRoute connections?

BGP is used in Azure Virtual Network Gateway to dynamically exchange route information between on-premises networks and Azure. It enables efficient routing and failover capabilities.

8.1.7 How does Azure Virtual Network Gateway support multi-site and active-active VPN configurations, and what are the benefits of these setups?

Azure Virtual Network Gateway supports multi-site VPN connections and active-active configurations, allowing multiple on-premises locations to connect to Azure simultaneously. This improves redundancy and load balancing.

8.1.8 What monitoring and troubleshooting tools are available for Azure Virtual Network Gateway, and how can administrators diagnose connectivity issues?

Azure Monitor and Azure Network Watcher provide monitoring and diagnostic capabilities for Virtual Network Gateways. These tools help identify and troubleshoot connectivity issues.

8.1.9 Can you describe the scenarios where Azure Virtual WAN complements Azure Virtual Network Gateway, and how does it simplify network management?

Azure Virtual WAN complements Virtual Network Gateway by simplifying network management for multiple Azure regions and providing optimized routing for branch offices. It's ideal for global enterprises.

8.1.10 What are the best practices for optimizing the performance and resilience of Azure Virtual Network Gateway, and how can organizations ensure high availability?
Best practices include choosing the appropriate gateway type, sizing resources correctly, implementing redundancy, and regularly monitoring and optimizing the configuration. High availability can be achieved through active-active configurations and geographic redundancy.

8.2 Azure Traffic Manager

8.2.1What is Azure Traffic Manager, and what is its primary purpose in a cloud environment?
Azure Traffic Manager is a DNS-based traffic load balancer that enables global distribution and high availability of applications hosted in different Azure regions or external endpoints. Its primary purpose is to improve application availability and responsiveness.

8.2.2 What are the various traffic-routing methods supported by Azure Traffic Manager, and when might you use each method?
Azure Traffic Manager supports several routing methods, including Priority, Weighted, Geographic, Performance, and Subnet. You might choose Priority for failover scenarios, Weighted for load balancing, Geographic for regional preference, Performance for low-latency routing, and Subnet for routing based on client IP addresses.

8.2.3 How does Azure Traffic Manager help with disaster recovery and application resilience?
Azure Traffic Manager can be configured with multiple endpoints in different Azure regions. In the event of a regional outage, it automatically routes traffic to the healthy region, ensuring high availability and minimizing downtime.

8.2.4 What are the key considerations for integrating Azure Traffic Manager with Azure services like Azure App Service or Azure Kubernetes Service (AKS)?
Integrating with Azure services is seamless, and you only need to provide the service's DNS name as an endpoint. However, you should consider health probe configurations, routing methods, and endpoint monitoring for optimal traffic management.

8.2.5 Can you explain how Azure Traffic Manager ensures the responsiveness and availability of endpoints, and what monitoring options are available?
Azure Traffic Manager periodically checks the health of endpoints using HTTP/HTTPS probes. When an endpoint becomes unhealthy, traffic is automatically rerouted to healthy endpoints. Additionally, Azure Monitor provides detailed metrics and monitoring capabilities to track the performance of Traffic Manager.

8.2.6 In what scenarios is Azure Traffic Manager particularly useful, and can you provide examples of how it can be applied to improve application performance and resilience?
Azure Traffic Manager is useful for scenarios where you need to distribute traffic across multiple geographic regions for global availability. Examples include load balancing web applications, content delivery, and disaster recovery setups.

8.2.7 How does Azure Traffic Manager handle endpoint types, including Azure endpoints, external endpoints, and nested Traffic Manager profiles?
Azure Traffic Manager supports different endpoint types, including Azure endpoints (Azure resources), external endpoints (external services), and nested Traffic Manager profiles (hierarchical configurations).

8.2.8 What security features are available in Azure Traffic Manager, and how can you secure DNS traffic and prevent DNS-based attacks?

Azure Traffic Manager supports DNS Security Extensions (DNSSEC) to secure DNS traffic. It also provides protection against DNS-based attacks, such as Distributed Denial of Service (DDoS) attacks.

8.2.9 What are the best practices for optimizing the performance and reliability of Azure Traffic Manager configurations, and how can organizations ensure minimal downtime during updates or changes?

Best practices include regularly monitoring and fine-tuning configurations, implementing geographic redundancy, using Azure Traffic Manager with Azure Availability Zones, and planning for minimal downtime during changes by leveraging features like Traffic View.

Top of Form

8.3 Azure ExpressRoute

8.3.1What is Azure ExpressRoute, and how does it differ from a traditional internet connection to Azure?

Azure ExpressRoute is a dedicated, private network connection service that allows organizations to connect their on-premises data centers to Azure. Unlike a traditional internet connection, ExpressRoute provides higher reliability, lower latency, and increased security for Azure workloads.

8.3.2What are the primary benefits of using Azure ExpressRoute for connecting on-premises networks to Azure?

ExpressRoute offers benefits such as predictable network performance, enhanced security through private connections, and the ability to meet compliance requirements. It also enables organizations to establish direct connectivity to Azure services, including Azure Virtual Networks and Azure SQL Database.

8.3.3 What are the different types of Azure ExpressRoute circuits, and how do they cater to various connectivity needs?

ExpressRoute offers two types of circuits: Standard and Premium. Standard circuits provide connectivity to Azure public services, while Premium circuits offer dedicated connectivity to Microsoft cloud services, including Azure, Office 365, and Dynamics 365.

8.3.4 Can you explain the concept of ExpressRoute peering, and why might organizations use Microsoft peering or private peering?

ExpressRoute peering allows connections to Microsoft's global network. Microsoft peering is used for accessing Microsoft public services like Azure PaaS and SaaS offerings. Private peering is used for accessing private IP addresses in Azure Virtual Networks.

8.3.5 How can organizations improve network redundancy and high availability with Azure ExpressRoute, and what are the considerations for achieving a resilient network architecture?

To achieve network redundancy and high availability, organizations can establish ExpressRoute connections in multiple Azure regions. Additionally, they should consider implementing ExpressRoute Global Reach to connect ExpressRoute circuits in different regions for enhanced resilience and failover capabilities.

8.3.6 How does Azure ExpressRoute integrate with Azure Virtual WAN, and what are the benefits of using this combination for network architecture?

Azure ExpressRoute can be connected to Azure Virtual WAN, simplifying network management and providing optimized routing for branch offices and remote locations, improving network architecture.

8.3.7 What security measures are in place to protect data transferred over an Azure ExpressRoute connection, and how is data encrypted?
Data transferred over Azure ExpressRoute is encrypted using industry-standard encryption protocols, ensuring data privacy and security. Additionally, Azure ExpressRoute supports Azure AD authentication and access control.

8.3.8 In what scenarios is Azure ExpressRoute with Microsoft peering used, and how does it enable organizations to securely access Azure public services?
Azure ExpressRoute with Microsoft peering is used when organizations need to access Azure public services like Azure Storage or Azure SQL Database privately and securely, without going over the public internet.

8.3.9 Can you describe the cost considerations for using Azure ExpressRoute, including the factors that impact pricing, and how organizations can optimize costs?
Azure ExpressRoute costs depend on factors like the chosen circuit type, data transfer volume, and location. To optimize costs, organizations can consider options like using ExpressRoute Direct or ExpressRoute Global Reach based on their needs.

ONLINE RESOURCES

Practice Paper
Link : https://forms.gle/gd6n6th5Kxr97WgY8

QR Code :

Video Content
Link : https://www.youtube.com/playlist?list=PLzlh_31VWEFooaIXkRIHSb-OLXUiyet6z

QR Code :

Chapter 9: Advanced Azure Topics

9.1 Azure DevOps and Continuous Integration/Continuous Deployment (CI/CD)

9.1.1 What is Azure DevOps, and how does it facilitate the software development lifecycle?
Azure DevOps is a set of development tools and services that support the entire software development lifecycle, including planning, coding, testing, and release management. It provides an integrated platform for collaboration, automation, and continuous delivery.

9.1.2 What is Continuous Integration (CI) and Continuous Deployment (CD), and why are they important in modern software development?
Continuous Integration (CI) is the practice of automatically building and testing code changes frequently. Continuous Deployment (CD) is the automated process of deploying code changes to production. They are crucial for improving code quality, reducing manual errors, and accelerating time-to-market.

9.1.3 How does Azure DevOps Pipelines support CI/CD, and what are the key components of a pipeline?
Azure DevOps Pipelines is a CI/CD service that enables the creation of automated build and release workflows. A pipeline consists of stages, jobs, and tasks. Stages define the sequence of actions, jobs run in parallel, and tasks execute specific actions like building, testing, or deploying.

9.1.4 Can you explain the concept of Infrastructure as Code (IaC) and its role in Azure DevOps CI/CD pipelines?
IaC is the practice of defining and provisioning infrastructure using code. In Azure DevOps, IaC templates (e.g., ARM templates or Terraform scripts) can be integrated into CI/CD pipelines to automate infrastructure provisioning alongside application deployment, ensuring consistent and reproducible environments.

9.1.5 How does Azure DevOps ensure security and compliance in CI/CD pipelines, and what security measures can be implemented?
Azure DevOps offers security features like role-based access control (RBAC), secure connections, secret management, and compliance checks. Security measures include scanning code for vulnerabilities, implementing secure coding practices, and adhering to regulatory requirements.

9.1.6 What are Blue-Green deployments and canary releases, and how can Azure DevOps support these deployment strategies?
Blue-Green deployments involve switching between two identical environments (blue and green) to minimize downtime during releases. Canary releases gradually expose new features to a subset of users. Azure DevOps can support these strategies by automating the deployment and monitoring of changes to ensure they meet performance and quality criteria.

9.1.7 What are some best practices for effective CI/CD pipeline design and management in Azure DevOps?
Best practices include defining clear pipeline stages, implementing automated testing, versioning code and artifacts, using infrastructure as code, setting up deployment gates, monitoring pipeline performance, and continuously improving through feedback and retrospectives.

9.1.8 How does Azure DevOps integrate with Azure Kubernetes Service (AKS) for container orchestration and deployment, and what are the benefits?
Azure DevOps integrates seamlessly with AKS to enable containerized application deployment. It automates container builds, testing, and deployment, making it easier to manage containerized applications at scale.

9.1.9 What are Blue-Green deployments and Feature Toggles in the context of Azure DevOps, and how do they support safe and controlled releases?
Blue-Green deployments involve running two identical environments (Blue and Green) and switching traffic to the newer one. Feature Toggles allow for selectively enabling or disabling features in production, reducing risk during deployment.
9.1.10 Can you describe the role of Azure DevOps Release Gates, and how do they enhance release quality and reliability?
Azure DevOps Release Gates are automated validation checks that occur during deployment. They can include performance tests, security scans, and other checks to ensure the release meets quality and reliability standards before reaching production.

9.2 Setting up Azure DevOps

9.2.1 What are the initial steps to set up Azure DevOps for a new project or organization?
To get started, create an Azure DevOps organization, define project structures, configure user access, and set up version control repositories. You can also establish initial build and release pipelines for CI/CD.
9.2.2 How does Azure DevOps handle user access and permissions, and what is the role of Azure Active Directory in user management?
Azure DevOps uses Azure Active Directory (Azure AD) for user authentication and access control. Administrators can assign roles and permissions to users or groups within Azure DevOps to control who can perform specific actions and access certain resources.
9.2.3 What are Azure DevOps Services and Azure DevOps Server, and how do they differ in terms of deployment options?
Azure DevOps Services is a cloud-based platform-as-a-service (PaaS) offering, while Azure DevOps Server is an on-premises, self-hosted solution. The primary difference lies in the deployment model: Services are hosted in the cloud, while Server is deployed in the organization's data center.
9.2.4 Can you explain the concept of Azure DevOps organizations and projects, and how they help manage multiple development efforts?
Azure DevOps organizations provide a logical separation for different development efforts, while projects offer a way to group related code repositories, build pipelines, and release pipelines within an organization. They help keep development efforts organized and isolated.
9.2.5 How can organizations integrate version control systems like Git with Azure DevOps, and what are the benefits of doing so?
Azure DevOps offers built-in support for Git repositories. Organizations can import existing Git repositories or create new ones directly within Azure DevOps. This integration enables version control, collaboration, and traceability for code changes.
9.2.6 What is the purpose of Azure DevOps artifacts, and how can organizations benefit from using a package management system?
Azure DevOps artifacts provide a package management system for storing and sharing software artifacts like libraries and packages. Organizations benefit by centralizing artifact storage, versioning, and distribution, which improves build and deployment consistency.
9.2.7 How does Azure DevOps support integration with other tools and services, and what are some common integrations that organizations might use?
Azure DevOps offers a rich ecosystem of extensions and integrations with popular tools and services, including CI/CD integrations, code analysis tools, issue tracking systems, and project

management software. These integrations enhance collaboration and automation across the software development lifecycle.

9.2.8 What are Azure Repos, and how can developers use them to manage and version control their code?

Azure Repos provide Git and Team Foundation Version Control (TFVC) repositories for code management. Developers can create, clone, and manage repositories to track code changes and collaborate with team members.

9.2.9 How can you extend Azure DevOps functionality through the Azure DevOps Marketplace, and what types of extensions are available?

The Azure DevOps Marketplace offers a wide range of extensions and integrations that enhance Azure DevOps functionality. These extensions include integrations with third-party tools, custom widgets, and more to tailor Azure DevOps to specific needs.

9.3 Building CI/CD Pipelines

9.3.1What is the purpose of a CI/CD pipeline, and how does it benefit the software development process?

A CI/CD pipeline automates the process of building, testing, and deploying code changes. It benefits development by improving code quality, reducing manual errors, accelerating development cycles, and enabling rapid and reliable releases.

9.3.2 Can you explain the key components of a typical CI/CD pipeline and their roles in the workflow?

A CI/CD pipeline typically includes stages for source code retrieval, building, testing, deploying, and monitoring. Components like triggers, jobs, and tasks define the actions performed in each stage, ensuring code changes are delivered smoothly.

9.3.3 What are the benefits of using version control systems like Git in a CI/CD pipeline, and how does it contribute to code quality?

Git allows versioning and collaboration, enabling developers to work on code changes in parallel. It also integrates seamlessly into CI/CD pipelines, automating the process of tracking changes, running tests, and deploying code, resulting in higher code quality.

9.3.4 How can organizations ensure security and compliance in CI/CD pipelines, especially when deploying to production environments?

Security and compliance can be ensured through practices such as automated security scanning, role-based access control (RBAC), and environment-specific configurations. Additionally, organizations should implement deployment gates and approval processes for production deployments.

9.3.5 What is the difference between a Blue-Green deployment and a Canary release in a CI/CD pipeline, and when might you use each strategy?

Blue-Green deployment involves switching traffic between two identical environments, minimizing downtime. Canary release gradually exposes new features to a subset of users. Blue-Green is suitable for minimizing downtime during critical updates, while Canary releases are ideal for gradual feature rollouts to assess user feedback and impact.

9.3.6 Can you explain the concept of Infrastructure as Code (IaC) in CI/CD pipelines, and how does it benefit automation and reproducibility?

IaC involves defining infrastructure using code, which can be versioned and automated in CI/CD pipelines. It benefits automation by allowing infrastructure provisioning alongside application deployment, ensuring consistent and reproducible environments throughout the development lifecycle.

9.3.7 How do CI/CD pipelines support rollback and recovery mechanisms in the event of deployment failures or issues in production?

CI/CD pipelines should include automated rollback mechanisms and health checks. In the event of deployment failures or issues in production, a pipeline can automatically trigger a rollback to the previous stable version, minimizing downtime and mitigating risks.

9.3.8 What are deployment strategies like Blue-Green and Canary deployments, and how do they enhance the reliability of code releases?

Blue-Green deployments involve switching traffic to a new environment (Blue to Green), while Canary deployments gradually roll out changes to a subset of users. These strategies minimize the risk of deploying faulty code to all users.

9.3.9 What are the best practices for securing and optimizing a CI/CD pipeline to ensure the confidentiality and integrity of the code and deployment process?

Best practices include securing pipeline secrets, using secure containers, implementing code scanning for vulnerabilities, and monitoring pipeline performance and security.

9.4 Monitoring and Logging

9.4.1 What is the importance of monitoring and logging in software applications, and how do they contribute to proactive issue resolution?

Monitoring and logging are crucial for detecting and diagnosing issues in real-time. They help in identifying performance bottlenecks, errors, and security threats, allowing teams to take proactive measures for issue resolution before they impact users.

9.4.2 Can you explain the difference between monitoring and logging, and how do they complement each other in troubleshooting and analysis?

Monitoring involves real-time tracking of system metrics and application performance, while logging records specific events and activities. Logging provides detailed context when troubleshooting issues detected by monitoring, making it easier to identify the root cause.

9.4.3 What are some key performance metrics that should be monitored in a production environment, and why are they important?

Key performance metrics include response time, throughput, error rates, and resource utilization. Monitoring these metrics helps ensure that the application meets performance expectations, maintains high availability, and delivers a positive user experience.

9.4.4 How does centralized logging using tools like ELK (Elasticsearch, Logstash, Kibana) or Azure Monitor Logs enhance troubleshooting and analysis capabilities?

Centralized logging consolidates logs from various sources into a single, searchable repository. Tools like ELK or Azure Monitor Logs provide powerful querying and visualization capabilities, simplifying troubleshooting and enabling historical analysis of issues.

9.4.5 What is alerting in the context of monitoring, and how can alerting rules be defined to notify teams of critical issues?

Alerting involves setting up rules based on defined thresholds or conditions to notify teams when specific events or issues occur. These rules can trigger notifications through various channels like email, SMS, or integration with incident management systems.

9.4.6 How can organizations ensure security and compliance through monitoring and logging practices, especially in regulated industries?

Organizations can implement security monitoring and logging to detect and respond to security threats. Compliance requirements often mandate retaining logs for a specific period and ensuring the security of sensitive data in logs.

9.4.7 What role does APM (Application Performance Monitoring) play in monitoring and logging, and how does it assist in optimizing application performance?

APM tools provide in-depth insights into application performance by tracing requests, identifying bottlenecks, and offering code-level visibility. They complement traditional monitoring and logging solutions, helping developers optimize application performance for better user experiences.

9.4.8 Can you explain the concept of anomaly detection in monitoring, and how machine learning can be used to identify abnormal behavior in cloud resources?

Anomaly detection involves using machine learning algorithms to identify deviations from normal resource behavior. This can help detect security breaches or performance issues.

9.4.9 How can organizations ensure the security and privacy of monitoring and logging data in a cloud environment, and what encryption and access control measures should be in place?

Organizations should use encryption for data in transit and at rest, implement access controls, and regularly audit access to monitoring and logging data to ensure security and privacy.

9.4.10 What cloud-native monitoring and logging solutions are available in popular cloud platforms like Azure, AWS, and Google Cloud, and how do they simplify the monitoring process?

Popular cloud platforms offer native monitoring and logging services like Azure Monitor, AWS CloudWatch, and Google Cloud Monitoring. These services simplify the setup and configuration of monitoring and logging, making it easier for organizations to gain insights into their cloud resources.

ONLINE RESOURCES

Practice Paper

Link : https://forms.gle/ERgQqT1rcXbj9sQj6

QR Code :

Video Content

Link : https://www.youtube.com/playlist?list=PLzlh_31VWEFqwP1IA7JXY-yFLLhCqXjN3

QR Code :

Chapter 10: Azure Security and Compliance

10.1 Azure Security Center

10.1.1 What is Azure Security Center, and what is its primary role in Azure cloud security?
Azure Security Center is a cloud-native security management system that helps organizations monitor and protect their Azure resources. Its primary role is to provide threat detection, security posture management, and security recommendations to enhance Azure cloud security.

10.1.2 How does Azure Security Center detect and respond to security threats and vulnerabilities in Azure environments?
Azure Security Center employs a combination of threat intelligence, behavioral analytics, and anomaly detection to identify security threats and vulnerabilities. It provides alerts and recommendations for remediation and integrates with Azure Monitor and Azure Sentinel for incident response.

10.1.3 Can you explain the concept of Azure Defender, and how it extends security coverage beyond Azure resources?
Azure Defender is an extension of Azure Security Center that provides advanced threat protection for resources both within and outside Azure. It extends security coverage to on-premises, multi-cloud, and hybrid environments, offering unified threat detection and response.

10.1.4 What are some common security recommendations and best practices that Azure Security Center provides to improve cloud security?
Azure Security Center offers recommendations for securing resources, including enabling firewall rules, implementing multi-factor authentication, applying vulnerability assessments, and maintaining secure configurations based on industry standards.

10.1.5 How does Azure Security Center assist with compliance and regulatory requirements, and what reporting capabilities are available?
Azure Security Center provides compliance assessments based on regulatory standards like GDPR, HIPAA, and NIST. It offers built-in reports and dashboards for monitoring compliance status and generating audit-ready reports.

10.1.6 What role does Threat Intelligence play in Azure Security Center, and how does it enhance threat detection?
Threat Intelligence in Azure Security Center provides insights into known threat indicators and attacker tactics, techniques, and procedures (TTPs). It enriches security alerts with contextual information, aiding security teams in understanding and responding to threats effectively.

10.1.7 Can you explain the integration options of Azure Security Center with other Azure services and third-party security solutions?
Azure Security Center integrates seamlessly with Azure services like Azure Monitor, Azure Sentinel, and Azure Logic Apps. It also offers connectors for third-party security solutions, enabling organizations to centralize their security operations and orchestrate responses.

10.1.8 Can you describe Azure Defender, and how does it enhance Azure Security Center's threat protection capabilities?
Azure Defender is an extension of Azure Security Center that provides advanced threat protection for Azure workloads and services. It includes features like network threat detection, container security, and SQL database threat detection.

10.1.9 How can organizations use Azure Security Center to gain visibility into their hybrid cloud environments, including on-premises resources?

Azure Security Center extends its protection to hybrid environments by using the Azure Arc feature, allowing organizations to monitor and secure on-premises servers, Kubernetes clusters, and other resources.

10.1.10 What are the best practices for configuring and using Azure Security Center to maximize the security benefits of the platform?

Best practices include enabling Azure Security Center for all subscriptions, regularly reviewing security recommendations, implementing multi-factor authentication, and setting up automated remediation for security alerts to ensure a proactive security stance.

10.2 Azure Policy

10.2.1 What is Azure Policy, and how does it contribute to Azure governance and compliance?

Azure Policy is a service that helps organizations enforce and monitor compliance with organizational standards and regulations in Azure. It enables governance by defining and enforcing policies for resource configurations.

10.2.2 How are Azure Policy definitions and assignments used to manage Azure resources, and what is their relationship?

Azure Policy definitions are the rules that specify what is allowed or denied for resources. Assignments are the instances where these definitions are applied to specific Azure scopes, such as management groups, subscriptions, or resource groups.

10.2.3 Can you explain the concept of built-in and custom policy definitions in Azure Policy, and when might organizations use each type?

Azure Policy provides built-in policy definitions that cover common compliance requirements. Custom policy definitions allow organizations to create tailored policies to meet specific business needs, ensuring flexibility and alignment with unique requirements.

10.2.4 How can Azure Policy be used to enforce resource tagging standards and naming conventions in an Azure environment?

Azure Policy can be used to enforce policies that require resources to have specific tags or adhere to naming conventions. This helps standardize resource naming and metadata for better organization and management.

10.2.5 What role does Azure Policy Guest Configuration play in ensuring the security of virtual machines, and how does it work?

Azure Policy Guest Configuration allows organizations to audit and enforce configurations within the guest operating systems of virtual machines. It relies on built-in or custom initiatives that define configuration settings and policies to ensure security compliance.

10.2.6 How does Azure Policy integrate with Azure DevOps and CI/CD pipelines to enforce policies during application deployment?

Azure Policy can be integrated into CI/CD pipelines through tools like Azure Resource Manager templates and ARM Template Checker tasks. This integration ensures that resource deployments conform to defined policies, preventing non-compliant configurations from being deployed.

10.2.7 What are the monitoring and reporting capabilities of Azure Policy, and how can organizations track policy compliance and violations?

Azure Policy provides monitoring through the Azure Portal, Azure Policy Compliance dashboard, and Azure Monitor. It offers detailed reports, alerts, and insights into policy compliance, allowing organizations to track and remediate violations effectively.

10.2.8 How can Azure Policy help organizations achieve compliance with regulatory standards such as GDPR, HIPAA, or PCI DSS?

Azure Policy allows organizations to create policies that align with specific regulatory requirements. By enforcing these policies, organizations can ensure that their Azure resources comply with the necessary standards.

10.2.9 What are the best practices for managing and organizing Azure Policy definitions and assignments in complex Azure environments?

Best practices include using naming conventions for policies, grouping policies into initiatives, and using Azure Blueprints for managing policy assignments at scale.

10.3 Data Encryption and Compliance

10.3.1 What is data encryption, and why is it essential for maintaining data security and compliance?

Data encryption is the process of converting data into a secure format to prevent unauthorized access. It is essential for data security and compliance as it safeguards sensitive information and helps meet regulatory requirements for data protection.

10.3.2 How does Azure Key Vault contribute to data encryption and compliance in Azure environments?

Azure Key Vault is a cloud service that enables the secure management of cryptographic keys, secrets, and certificates. It helps maintain data encryption by providing a central location for key management and supports compliance by facilitating key rotation and audit logging.

10.3.3 Can you explain the difference between encryption in transit and encryption at rest, and why both are important for securing data?

Encryption in transit ensures data is secured while being transmitted over networks, while encryption at rest safeguards data stored on storage devices or databases. Both are crucial for data security because they protect data during transmission and storage, reducing the risk of data breaches.

10.3.4 How does Azure Disk Encryption enhance data security and compliance for virtual machines in Azure?

Azure Disk Encryption encrypts the OS and data disks of Azure virtual machines using industry-standard encryption mechanisms. It helps maintain data security and compliance by protecting sensitive data stored on virtual disks, ensuring data confidentiality.

10.3.5 What is the role of Azure Information Protection in data classification, labeling, and protection, and how can it assist with compliance efforts?

Azure Information Protection allows organizations to classify, label, and protect sensitive data based on predefined policies. It assists with compliance by automatically applying data protection measures, such as encryption and access controls, to ensure data is handled in accordance with regulatory requirements.

10.3.6 How can organizations use Azure Security Center to assess data security and compliance posture, and what recommendations does it provide?

Azure Security Center offers continuous monitoring and assessments of data security. It provides recommendations and best practices for data encryption, access control, and compliance, helping organizations improve their security posture.

10.3.7 What are some common compliance frameworks and regulations that organizations must adhere to, and how can Azure services and tools assist in achieving compliance?

Common compliance frameworks include GDPR, HIPAA, PCI DSS, and ISO 27001. Azure provides compliance offerings and documentation that align with these frameworks, allowing organizations to leverage Azure services and tools to help meet compliance requirements and audit obligations.

10.3.8 Can you explain the concept of data residency and data sovereignty, and why they are important considerations for organizations in a global cloud environment?

Data residency refers to the physical location where data is stored, while data sovereignty refers to the legal jurisdiction governing that data. These considerations are important for ensuring that data complies with regional data protection laws and regulations.

10.3.9 What is the Shared Responsibility Model in cloud security, and how does it apply to data encryption and compliance in Azure?

The Shared Responsibility Model outlines the division of security responsibilities between cloud providers and customers. While Azure ensures the security of the cloud infrastructure, customers are responsible for securing their data and configurations.

ONLINE RESOURCES

Practice Paper
Link : https://forms.gle/YrBUx8GAifiHMQL39

QR Code :

Video Content
Link : https://www.youtube.com/playlist?list=PLzlh_31VWEFofP0s7WR8xKlSnslKQj17G

QR Code :

Chapter 11: Azure Hybrid Cloud and Integration

11.1 Azure Logic Apps

11.1.1 What is Azure Logic Apps, and how does it differ from other integration services in Azure?

Azure Logic Apps is a cloud-based service that enables workflow automation and integration between various applications and services. It differs from other services like Azure Functions or Azure Web Jobs by focusing on visual, low-code/no-code workflows for automating business processes.

11.1.2 Can you explain the key components of an Azure Logic App workflow, and how do triggers and actions work together?

An Azure Logic App consists of triggers and actions. Triggers initiate the workflow based on an event, and actions perform specific tasks. Triggers and actions work together to automate processes, such as sending emails, processing data, or updating databases.

11.1.3 What are some common use cases for Azure Logic Apps, and how can organizations benefit from using them?

Azure Logic Apps can be used for a wide range of scenarios, including integration with SaaS applications, data synchronization, notification workflows, and IoT data processing. Organizations benefit from increased productivity, reduced manual tasks, and streamlined business processes.

11.1.4 How does Azure Logic Apps integrate with other Azure services and external systems, and what connectors are available for different integrations?

Azure Logic Apps offers a vast array of connectors to integrate with Azure services, third-party applications, and on-premises systems. It can connect to services like Azure Storage, Office 365, Salesforce, and more through these connectors.

11.1.5 What is the role of workflows in Azure Logic Apps, and how can they be designed and customized to meet specific business requirements?

Workflows in Azure Logic Apps define the sequence of steps to accomplish a task. They can be designed visually using Logic App Designer or through code using Azure Resource Manager templates. Workflows are highly customizable and can include branching, loops, and error handling.

11.1.6 How does Azure Logic Apps ensure reliability and scalability for mission-critical workflows, and what monitoring and diagnostics features are available?

Azure Logic Apps offers built-in reliability through automatic retries and parallel execution. It also provides monitoring capabilities, such as tracking the execution history, capturing diagnostics logs, and integrating with Azure Monitor for advanced monitoring and alerting.

11.1.7 Can you explain the pricing model for Azure Logic Apps, and what factors should organizations consider when estimating costs?

Azure Logic Apps are billed based on the number of workflow executions and connector actions. Organizations should consider the complexity of their workflows, the frequency of executions, and the number of actions when estimating costs. Azure Logic Apps also offer a consumption-based pricing model for cost optimization.

11.1.8 What is the role of triggers in Azure Logic Apps, and can you provide examples of trigger types that can initiate workflows?

Triggers are events that start Logic App workflows. Examples of trigger types include "When a new email arrives," "When an HTTP request is received," and "When a file is created or modified."

11.1.9 How can Azure Logic Apps be monitored and audited to ensure proper functioning and identify potential issues?

Azure Logic Apps can be monitored through Azure Monitor and Azure Application Insights. These services provide insights into workflow execution, performance, and error tracking.

11.1.10 What are best practices for securing Azure Logic Apps, including authentication, access control, and data protection?

Best practices include using Azure Active Directory authentication, implementing role-based access control (RBAC), encrypting sensitive data, and following Azure security recommendations to protect Logic Apps and the data they process.

11.2 Hybrid Cloud Deployment Models

11.2.1 What is a Hybrid Cloud Deployment Model, and why do organizations choose to implement it?

A Hybrid Cloud Deployment Model combines both on-premises infrastructure and cloud services to create a unified computing environment. Organizations adopt this model to leverage the scalability and flexibility of the cloud while maintaining control over critical data and applications hosted on-premises.

11.2.2 Can you explain the difference between a Hybrid Cloud and a Multi-Cloud deployment model, and when might each be preferred?

A Hybrid Cloud combines on-premises and cloud resources from a single cloud provider, while a Multi-Cloud strategy involves using multiple cloud providers simultaneously. Organizations may choose Hybrid Cloud for simplicity and cost savings, while Multi-Cloud provides flexibility and avoids vendor lock-in.

11.2.3 What are some common Hybrid Cloud deployment patterns, such as Hybrid IaaS, Hybrid PaaS, and Hybrid SaaS, and how do they enable different use cases?

Hybrid IaaS combines on-premises infrastructure with cloud-based virtual machines. Hybrid PaaS integrates on-premises and cloud platforms for application development, while Hybrid SaaS allows users to access software both on-premises and via the cloud, catering to various business needs.

11.2.4 How can organizations ensure data consistency and synchronization between on-premises and cloud environments in a Hybrid Cloud deployment?

Organizations can use data replication and synchronization tools to ensure data consistency. Technologies like Azure Site Recovery, Azure Data Factory, and Azure SQL Data Sync facilitate data movement and synchronization in Hybrid Cloud deployments.

11.2.5 What role does Identity and Access Management (IAM) play in Hybrid Cloud deployments, and how can organizations maintain secure access?

IAM is crucial for managing user access across hybrid environments. Organizations can use Azure Active Directory (Azure AD) and other identity management solutions to enforce secure access controls, Single Sign-On (SSO), and Multi-Factor Authentication (MFA) for hybrid resources.

11.2.6 How does a Hybrid Cloud deployment model enhance disaster recovery and business continuity planning?

Hybrid Cloud provides redundancy and failover options between on-premises and cloud environments, ensuring that critical workloads can be quickly recovered in the event of disasters. Azure Site Recovery, for instance, offers robust disaster recovery capabilities for Hybrid Cloud deployments.

11.2.7 What challenges do organizations face when implementing a Hybrid Cloud deployment model, and how can they overcome these challenges?
Challenges may include data security concerns, complex network configurations, and management overhead. Organizations can address these challenges by implementing robust security measures, designing efficient network connectivity, and using cloud management tools like Azure Arc to simplify hybrid operations.
11.2.8 How does a hybrid cloud deployment impact an organization's network architecture, and what networking solutions are available to connect on-premises and cloud resources?
Hybrid cloud requires a robust network architecture with VPNs, ExpressRoute, or direct connections to establish secure and high-performance connections between on-premises and cloud environments.
11.2.9 What role does compliance play in hybrid cloud deployments, and how can organizations ensure they meet regulatory requirements when using both on-premises and cloud resources?
Compliance is critical in hybrid cloud. Organizations must ensure that both on-premises and cloud environments meet regulatory standards by implementing encryption, access controls, and auditing.
11.2.10 How can organizations maintain cost efficiency in a hybrid cloud model, and what cost management strategies should be employed to optimize spending?
Cost efficiency can be achieved through careful resource allocation, monitoring, and the use of cloud cost management tools. Organizations should regularly assess their resource utilization to identify cost-saving opportunities.

11.3 Azure Hybrid Integration Services

11.3.1 What are Azure Hybrid Integration Services, and why are they essential for organizations with hybrid IT environments?
Azure Hybrid Integration Services are a set of Azure services that enable seamless communication and integration between on-premises systems and cloud applications. They are essential for organizations to bridge the gap between legacy on-premises infrastructure and modern cloud solutions, ensuring smooth data and application integration.
11.3.2 Can you explain the role of Azure Logic Apps and Azure Service Bus in Azure Hybrid Integration Services, and how do they facilitate data and application integration?
Azure Logic Apps provide workflow automation and orchestration capabilities, making it easy to design and automate integration workflows between on-premises and cloud systems. Azure Service Bus offers reliable messaging and event-driven communication, allowing for real-time data exchange and event processing.
11.3.3 What is Azure API Management, and how can it enhance API integration in hybrid environments?
Azure API Management is a fully managed service that enables organizations to publish, secure, and manage APIs. It plays a crucial role in hybrid integration by allowing organizations to expose and manage APIs securely, making it easier for on-premises and cloud systems to communicate via APIs.
11.3.4 How can Azure Hybrid Connections simplify secure access to on-premises resources from Azure services, and what scenarios benefit from this capability?
Azure Hybrid Connections provide a secure and simple way to establish connections between Azure services and on-premises systems without requiring complex networking configurations.

Scenarios such as accessing on-premises databases, files, or web services benefit from this capability.

11.3.5 What is the purpose of Azure Data Factory in hybrid integration, and how does it support data integration and transformation between on-premises and cloud data sources?

Azure Data Factory is a data integration service that orchestrates and automates data movement and transformation. It helps organizations integrate data from various on-premises and cloud sources, enabling data-driven insights and analytics in hybrid environments.

11.3.6 How can organizations ensure security and compliance when using Azure Hybrid Integration Services, especially when dealing with sensitive on-premises data?

Security and compliance can be maintained through identity and access management, encryption, and auditing. Azure services like Azure AD, Azure Key Vault, and Azure Security Center help organizations protect data and ensure compliance with industry standards.

11.3.7 What monitoring and troubleshooting tools are available for Azure Hybrid Integration Services, and how can they help organizations maintain operational visibility and performance?

Azure Monitor and Azure Application Insights provide monitoring and diagnostics capabilities for tracking the health and performance of integration workflows. They offer insights, alerts, and analytics to ensure optimal operation of hybrid integration solutions.

11.3.8 What are some best practices for securing data and communication in hybrid integration scenarios, considering the exchange of sensitive information?

Best practices include implementing encryption, securing access with Azure AD, monitoring for security threats, and adhering to compliance standards such as HIPAA and GDPR.

11.3.9 What are the key considerations for selecting the right Azure Hybrid Integration Services components and architecture to meet specific integration needs?

Consider factors such as the type of applications, data volume, performance requirements, and existing infrastructure when selecting the appropriate Azure Hybrid Integration Services components and architecture for a given integration project.

11.4 Hybrid Cloud Security and Governance

11.4.1 What are the key security challenges organizations face when implementing a Hybrid Cloud model, and how can they address them?

Security challenges in Hybrid Cloud include data protection, identity management, and compliance. To address them, organizations should implement encryption, use robust identity and access management tools, and establish policies for compliance across on-premises and cloud environments.

11.4.2 How does Azure Policy assist organizations in maintaining security and governance in Hybrid Cloud deployments?

Azure Policy enables organizations to define and enforce specific security and compliance rules across their Azure resources. This ensures that resources in both on-premises and cloud environments adhere to organizational standards, enhancing security and governance.

11.4.3 Can you explain the role of Azure Blueprints in ensuring compliance and governance in Hybrid Cloud environments?

Azure Blueprints enable organizations to define a repeatable set of resources and policies for various scenarios. They help ensure compliance by consistently deploying compliant resources and configurations across both on-premises and Azure environments.

11.4.4 What best practices should organizations follow to secure data transmission and communication between on-premises and Azure environments in a Hybrid Cloud setup?

To secure data transmission, organizations should implement Virtual Private Network (VPN) connections, use ExpressRoute for dedicated private connections, and enforce encryption protocols, such as TLS/SSL, for data in transit.

11.4.5 How does Azure Security Center assist in monitoring and protecting Hybrid Cloud environments, and what types of threats does it detect?

Azure Security Center provides threat detection and security monitoring across on-premises and Azure resources. It detects threats like malware, suspicious activities, and vulnerabilities, offering recommendations and alerts for timely response.

11.4.6 What are the benefits of using Azure Monitor and Azure Sentinel for hybrid cloud security and governance, and how do they complement each other?

Azure Monitor provides real-time monitoring and log analytics, while Azure Sentinel offers advanced security information and event management (SIEM) capabilities. Together, they provide comprehensive visibility, detection, and response for security and governance across hybrid environments.

11.4.7 How can organizations balance the need for security and governance with the flexibility and agility offered by Hybrid Cloud deployments?

Organizations should adopt a risk-based approach to security, leveraging automation and policy-driven governance to strike a balance between security and agility. Regular risk assessments, compliance audits, and proactive monitoring can help maintain this balance effectively.

11.4.8 How do hybrid cloud security and governance practices support the scalability and flexibility benefits of hybrid cloud models?

Security and governance practices ensure that scalability and flexibility do not compromise the security and compliance of hybrid environments. They enable organizations to grow while adhering to regulatory requirements.

11.4.9 What are some best practices for organizations looking to establish a robust hybrid cloud security and governance strategy?

Best practices include conducting risk assessments, implementing a comprehensive security framework, regularly auditing configurations, educating staff on security policies, and staying informed about emerging threats and compliance changes.

ONLINE RESOURCES

Practice Paper

Link : https://forms.gle/6BUCR1XrBvU2gNVa6

QR Code :

Video Content

Link :

https://www.youtube.com/playlist?list=PLzlh_31VWEFpFr6T1ebeeXHEAxVIr21B4

QR Code :

Chapter 12: Azure Data Factory

12.1 Data Movement and Integration

12.1.1 What is data integration, and why is it important in modern business environments?
Data integration is the process of combining data from different sources into a single, unified view. It's essential as it enables organizations to make informed decisions, enhance operational efficiency, and gain insights from diverse data sources.

12.1.2 Can you explain the difference between ETL (Extract, Transform, Load) and ELT (Extract, Load, Transform) data integration approaches?
ETL extracts data from source systems, transforms it, and then loads it into the target system. ELT extracts data first, loads it into a target system, and then performs transformations. ELT is often used when the target system can handle data transformations efficiently.

12.1.3 What are common data integration challenges, and how can organizations address them effectively?
Challenges include data silos, data quality issues, and handling real-time data. Organizations can address these challenges by implementing data governance practices, using integration platforms, and employing data quality tools.

12.1.4 How does Azure Data Factory facilitate data movement and transformation in cloud environments, and what are its key components?
Azure Data Factory is a cloud-based data integration service that enables data movement and transformation. Its components include pipelines, datasets, activities, and linked services, which work together to orchestrate data workflows.

12.1.5 What role does Azure Logic Apps play in integrating data and services across various applications and platforms?
Azure Logic Apps are used to create workflows that automate the integration of data and services. They can connect to a wide range of services and applications, making it easier to orchestrate data movement and integration tasks.

12.1.6 Can you explain the purpose of Azure Data Lake Storage and Azure SQL Data Warehouse in data movement and analytics?
Azure Data Lake Storage is a scalable data lake solution for storing and analyzing large volumes of data. Azure SQL Data Warehouse is a fully managed, cloud-based data warehouse service optimized for analytics. Together, they support data movement, storage, and analytics tasks.

12.1.7 What is Azure Data Factory Data Flow, and how does it simplify data transformation processes?
Azure Data Factory Data Flow is a cloud-based data transformation service that enables ETL and data wrangling tasks. It provides a visual interface for building data transformations without the need for complex coding.

12.1.8 How can organizations ensure data security and compliance when moving and integrating data across cloud and on-premises environments?

Data security and compliance can be ensured through encryption, access controls, data masking, and compliance monitoring tools. Azure offers robust security features and compliance certifications to help organizations meet regulatory requirements.

12.1.9 What is the significance of data integration for business intelligence and reporting, and how does it improve decision-making?

Data integration ensures that accurate and up-to-date data is available for business intelligence (BI) and reporting tools. It enables organizations to generate insights, create dashboards, and make data-driven decisions, ultimately improving business outcomes.

12.2 Data Orchestration

12.2.1 What is data orchestration, and how does it differ from traditional data integration?

Data orchestration involves coordinating and automating data workflows across various sources, transformations, and destinations. It differs from traditional data integration by emphasizing the dynamic and flexible nature of data movement and processing.

12.2.2 Can you explain the concept of data pipelines and how they are used in data orchestration?

Data pipelines are sequences of data processing and movement tasks orchestrated to achieve specific objectives. They are used in data orchestration to define, automate, and monitor data workflows, ensuring data flows efficiently through various stages.

12.2.3 What role does Azure Data Factory play in data orchestration, and how does it simplify the creation of data pipelines?

Azure Data Factory is a cloud-based data integration service that enables data orchestration. It simplifies the creation of data pipelines through a visual interface, making it easy to design, schedule, and monitor data workflows.

12.2.4 How can organizations ensure data orchestration tasks are executed in the correct order and handle dependencies between tasks effectively?

Data orchestration tools like Azure Data Factory support defining task dependencies and orchestrating their execution based on dependencies. This ensures that tasks run in the correct order and maintain data integrity.

12.2.5 What is the significance of data triggers in data orchestration, and how do they enable automation and scheduling?

Data triggers in data orchestration tools allow for the automation and scheduling of data workflows. They enable tasks to be executed based on predefined conditions or time-based schedules, ensuring timely data processing.

12.2.6 How does data orchestration help in managing and automating data movement between on-premises and cloud environments?

Data orchestration tools can connect to on-premises and cloud data sources and destinations. They enable organizations to automate data movement, transformations, and synchronization seamlessly across hybrid environments.

12.2.7 What are some common challenges organizations face in data orchestration, and how can they overcome these challenges?

Challenges include handling data latency, ensuring data quality, and managing complex data workflows. Organizations can address these challenges by optimizing pipeline design, implementing data validation, and using monitoring and alerting solutions.

12.2.8 How does data orchestration enhance data governance and compliance, especially when dealing with sensitive data?

Data orchestration can enforce data governance policies, data masking, and access controls. It helps organizations maintain compliance with data protection regulations by ensuring that sensitive data is handled securely.

12.2.9 Can you explain the concept of error handling and retry mechanisms in data orchestration, and why are they important?

Error handling and retry mechanisms in data orchestration tools help manage issues that may arise during data workflows, such as network interruptions or data source unavailability. They are important for ensuring data pipelines are robust and reliable.

12.2.10 How can organizations leverage data orchestration to achieve scalability and flexibility in their data processing workflows?

Data orchestration tools provide scalability by allowing organizations to scale data processing resources as needed. They also offer flexibility to adapt to changing data requirements and business needs by enabling easy modification of data pipelines.

12.3 Data Sources and Destinations

12.3.1 What are data sources and data destinations in the context of data integration, and why are they important?

Data sources are the locations or systems from which data is extracted, while data destinations are where data is loaded or delivered. They are essential for data integration as they define the origin and destination of data flows.

12.3.2 What are some common types of data sources in data integration, and can you provide examples of each?

Common data sources include databases (e.g., SQL Server, Oracle), cloud services (e.g., Azure Blob Storage, AWS S3), web services (e.g., REST APIs), flat files (e.g., CSV, JSON), and IoT devices (e.g., sensors).

12.3.3 How can organizations ensure data quality when extracting data from various sources, especially when dealing with heterogeneous data formats?

Ensuring data quality involves data cleansing, transformation, and validation. Data integration tools often provide data profiling and transformation capabilities to address data quality issues during extraction.

12.3.4 What are data destinations typically used for in data integration, and how do they enable efficient data storage and analysis?

Data destinations are used to store, process, and analyze data. They enable organizations to consolidate data from various sources for reporting, analytics, and business intelligence purposes.

12.3.5 Can you explain the importance of data mapping and schema transformations when moving data between sources and destinations?

Data mapping defines how data from source systems is transformed into a format compatible with the destination. Schema transformations ensure data consistency and alignment between source and destination schemas.

12.3.6 What are the challenges organizations may encounter when integrating data from cloud-based sources into on-premises data warehouses or vice versa?

Challenges may include network latency, data security, and data synchronization. Organizations should implement hybrid integration solutions to address these challenges effectively.

12.3.7 How do data integration platforms like Azure Data Factory or Apache NiFi simplify the process of connecting to diverse data sources and destinations?

Data integration platforms provide connectors and adapters to interact with a wide range of data sources and destinations. They offer a centralized interface for designing, managing, and monitoring data integration workflows.

12.3.8 What is data replication, and how can it be used to maintain data consistency between source and destination systems?

Data replication involves copying data from a source to a destination in real-time or near-real-time. It ensures data consistency by keeping the destination system synchronized with changes in the source.

12.3.9 How can organizations ensure data security and compliance when transferring sensitive data between data sources and destinations?

Data encryption, access controls, and auditing are essential measures for data security and compliance. Using secure protocols and identity management solutions also helps protect sensitive data during transit.

12.4 Data Transformation and Data Flows

12.4.1 What is data transformation, and why is it a crucial step in the data integration process?

Data transformation is the process of converting and altering data from its source format into a format suitable for the destination system. It's vital as it ensures data consistency, quality, and compatibility.

12.4.2 How can organizations handle schema changes and data type conversions effectively during data transformation processes?

Effective data transformation tools and processes allow organizations to handle schema changes by mapping source and destination fields and managing data type conversions based on defined rules.

12.4.3 Can you explain the difference between batch data transformation and real-time data transformation, and when might each be preferred?

Batch data transformation processes data in fixed batches or intervals, while real-time transformation processes data as it arrives. Batch transformation is suitable for non-time-sensitive tasks, whereas real-time transformation is ideal for immediate data processing requirements.

12.4.4 What role do data transformation functions and expressions play in defining data transformations, and can you provide examples of common transformations?

Data transformation functions and expressions define how data is modified during transformation. Examples include data formatting, aggregation, filtering, and calculations like sum, average, or date conversions.

12.4.5 How does data mapping facilitate data transformation, and what are the key considerations when designing data mappings?

Data mapping defines the relationship between source and destination fields, specifying how data is mapped and transformed. Key considerations include field compatibility, data validation, and handling missing or erroneous data.

12.4.6 What are data transformation pipelines, and how do they help organizations orchestrate complex data transformation processes?

Data transformation pipelines are sequences of data transformation steps executed in a defined order. They help organizations structure and automate complex data transformations, ensuring data flows through multiple stages efficiently.

12.4.7 How can data transformation tools handle unstructured or semi-structured data, such as text or JSON files, and integrate them into structured databases?

Data transformation tools provide parsing and extraction capabilities to convert unstructured or semi-structured data into structured formats. For example, JSON data can be parsed and mapped to relational database tables.

12.4.8 What is data enrichment, and how does it enhance the value of transformed data?

Data enrichment involves enhancing data by adding supplementary information, such as geolocation data or external reference data. It improves data quality and enables more comprehensive analytics and reporting.

12.4.9 How do organizations ensure data lineage and auditability during data transformation processes, especially in regulated industries?

Organizations maintain data lineage by tracking the history and transformations of data. Audit trails and metadata records capture information about who performed transformations, when, and why, ensuring transparency and compliance.

12.4.10 What are the performance considerations when designing data transformation workflows, and how can organizations optimize data transformation for efficiency?

Performance considerations include data volume, processing speed, and resource utilization. To optimize data transformation, organizations can parallelize processing, use caching mechanisms, and choose appropriate hardware or cloud resources based on workload requirements.

ONLINE RESOURCES

Practice Paper

Link : https://forms.gle/so4YsveMCHAgGVRM7

QR Code :

Video Content

Link :

https://www.youtube.com/playlist?list=PLzlh_31VWEFpGxBhfZGwv4vpZFV2PjsMt

QR Code :

Chapter 13: Azure Databricks

13.1 Introduction to Azure Databricks

13.1.1 What is Azure Databricks, and how does it differ from traditional Apache Spark?
Azure Databricks is a cloud-based big data analytics and machine learning platform. It enhances Apache Spark by offering a collaborative and fully managed environment with integrated Azure services for data processing and AI.

13.1.2 What are the primary use cases for Azure Databricks, and how can organizations benefit from using it?
Azure Databricks is used for data exploration, data engineering, advanced analytics, and machine learning. Organizations benefit from improved productivity, faster insights, and simplified data workflows.

13.1.3 How does Azure Databricks facilitate collaboration among data scientists, data engineers, and business analysts?
Azure Databricks provides a collaborative workspace where users can create and share notebooks, collaborate on code, and visualize data together. This fosters cross-functional collaboration within organizations.

13.1.4 What are the key components of Azure Databricks, and how do they work together to enable data analytics and processing?
The key components include the Databricks Workspace, Databricks Runtime, and integrated Azure services. The Workspace provides a unified interface, while the Runtime offers optimized Spark clusters for data processing. Integrated Azure services enhance functionality.

13.1.5 How does Azure Databricks help organizations accelerate time-to-insight and reduce the complexity of data processing tasks?
Azure Databricks automates many aspects of data processing, such as cluster management and optimization, allowing users to focus on data analysis and machine learning. This accelerates insights and reduces operational complexity.

13.1.6 Can you explain the role of Databricks Notebooks in Azure Databricks, and how do they support data exploration and analysis?
Databricks Notebooks are interactive and collaborative environments for writing code, visualizing data, and documenting analysis. They support data exploration by allowing users to interactively query and visualize data in real-time.

13.1.7 What Azure services can be integrated with Azure Databricks, and how does this integration enhance data analytics capabilities?
Azure Databricks seamlessly integrates with Azure services like Azure Storage, Azure SQL Data Warehouse, and Azure Machine Learning. This integration enables data ingestion, storage, and advanced analytics, creating a comprehensive data analytics ecosystem.

13.2 Azure Databricks Architecture

13.2.1 Can you describe the high-level architecture of Azure Databricks and its components?
Azure Databricks architecture consists of clusters for computation, the Databricks Workspace for collaboration, and integration with Azure services. It combines the Databricks control plane and the Azure cloud infrastructure.

13.2.2 What is the purpose of Databricks clusters, and how does Azure Databricks optimize cluster management?

Databricks clusters are used for distributed data processing. Azure Databricks optimizes cluster management by offering autoscaling, auto-termination, and cluster policies to minimize opcrational ovcrhcad.

13.2.3 How does Azure Databricks leverage Azure Virtual Network integration to enhance data security and privacy?

Azure Databricks allows customers to deploy clusters within their Azure Virtual Network (VNet). This enhances data security by isolating Databricks workloads and enabling secure communication with on-premises resources.

13.2.4 What is the role of the Databricks Runtime in Azure Databricks, and how does it simplify Spark cluster management?

Databricks Runtime is a version of Apache Spark optimized for Azure Databricks. It simplifies cluster management by providing pre-configured environments, libraries, and optimizations for efficient data processing.

13.2.5 How does the integration of the Databricks Workspace with Azure Active Directory (Azure AD) enhance identity and access management in Azure Databricks?

Integration with Azure AD enables fine-grained access control, Single Sign-On (SSO), and Multi-Factor Authentication (MFA) for users of the Databricks Workspace, ensuring secure collaboration and data access.

13.2.6 How does the collaborative nature of Azure Databricks, with features like notebooks and version control, enhance data analytics projects?

Collaborative features enable data scientists and engineers to work together within a unified environment. Notebooks provide a platform for sharing code and visualizations, while version control ensures project traceability and collaboration.

13.3 Data Processing with Azure Databricks

13.3.1 How does Azure Databricks handle data ingestion from various sources, and what are some supported data ingestion methods?

Azure Databricks supports various data ingestion methods, including batch data loading from Azure Data Lake Storage and Azure Blob Storage, streaming data ingestion from sources like Azure Event Hubs, and direct connectivity to databases like Azure SQL Data Warehouse.

13.3.2 Can you explain the concept of Delta Lake in Azure Databricks and its role in ensuring data reliability and consistency?

Delta Lake is a storage layer that brings ACID transactional capabilities to data lakes. It ensures data reliability and consistency by providing features like asset transactions, schema evolution, and time travel for data versioning.

13.3.3 What is the significance of data transformation in Azure Databricks, and how can data engineers and data scientists leverage it for data processing?

Data transformation in Azure Databricks involves preparing, cleaning, and structuring data for analysis. Data engineers and data scientists can use Spark-based transformations to refine raw data into a format suitable for analytics, machine learning, and reporting.

13.3.4 How does Azure Databricks support real-time data processing and analytics, and what types of use cases benefit from real-time data streaming?

Azure Databricks integrates with streaming sources like Azure Event Hubs and Apache Kafka to enable real-time data processing. Use cases include fraud detection, IoT analytics, monitoring, and personalized recommendations.

13.3.5 What is the role of Databricks jobs in automating and scheduling data processing tasks, and how can they be configured in Azure Databricks?
Databricks jobs automate the execution of notebooks and workflows. They can be configured to run on a schedule, trigger data processing tasks, and send notifications upon completion, streamlining data processing operations.
13.3.6 How does Azure Databricks support data visualization and reporting, and what are some integrated tools for creating data visualizations?
Azure Databricks allows users to create data visualizations within notebooks using libraries like Matplotlib and Seaborn. Additionally, it integrates with Power BI and other BI tools for advanced reporting and visualization.
13.3.7 What are the advantages of using Databricks Delta for data storage and processing, and how does it simplify data pipeline development in Azure Databricks?
Databricks Delta provides ACID transaction support, schema enforcement, and data versioning, which enhance data reliability and simplify pipeline development. It ensures data consistency and makes data pipelines more robust and manageable.

13.4 Azure Databricks Workflows

13.4.1 What are Databricks notebooks, and how do they play a central role in Azure Databricks workflows?
Databricks notebooks are interactive, web-based environments where users can create and share code, visualizations, and documentation. They are at the core of Azure Databricks workflows, enabling data scientists and engineers to collaborate and execute data processing tasks.
13.4.2 How can Azure Databricks notebooks be versioned and shared among team members to support collaborative data analysis?
Azure Databricks notebooks can be versioned using integrated version control systems like Git. They can also be shared with team members, allowing for collaborative analysis, code reviews, and documentation updates.
13.4.3 What is the purpose of Databricks jobs in Azure Databricks workflows, and how can they be scheduled and configured?
Databricks jobs automate the execution of notebooks and workflows. They can be scheduled to run at specific intervals or triggered based on events. Configuration options include specifying the cluster, notebook, parameters, and notification settings.
13.4.4 How does Azure Databricks support parameterization of notebooks, and why is this feature important for workflow flexibility?
Azure Databricks allows users to parameterize notebooks, making workflows flexible and reusable. Parameters enable the same notebook to be executed with different inputs or configurations, enhancing adaptability to changing requirements.
13.4.5 What is the significance of Databricks libraries and how do they extend the functionality of Azure Databricks notebooks?
Databricks libraries are additional Python or Scala packages that can be installed and used in notebooks. They extend the functionality of notebooks by providing access to external libraries, custom code, and connectors to various data sources and services.
13.4.6 What are the options for exporting and sharing results generated within Azure Databricks notebooks, and how can data insights be communicated effectively?

Azure Databricks notebooks offer export options for sharing results in various formats, such as HTML, PDF, and IPython. Users can also publish notebooks as dashboards or reports, making it easy to communicate data insights with stakeholders.

13.5 Advanced Analytics with Azure Databricks

13.5.1 How does Azure Databricks support machine learning and advanced analytics, and what are the key components of its machine learning ecosystem?

Azure Databricks provides a comprehensive machine learning ecosystem, including libraries like Scikit-learn and MLlib, and integration with Azure Machine Learning. It enables data scientists to build, train, and deploy machine learning models within the Databricks environment.

13.5.2 Can you explain the concept of distributed deep learning in Azure Databricks and how it can be used for training complex neural networks?

Distributed deep learning in Azure Databricks leverages distributed computing resources to accelerate the training of deep neural networks. Users can harness the power of distributed clusters to train complex models efficiently.

13.5.3 What is the significance of Databricks Delta in machine learning pipelines, and how does it contribute to data versioning and model tracking?

Databricks Delta ensures data versioning and transactional capabilities in machine learning pipelines. It allows data scientists to track changes in data and models, ensuring reproducibility and auditability in advanced analytics workflows.

13.5.4 How does Azure Databricks facilitate real-time data analytics and streaming analytics, and what are some use cases for real-time analytics?

Azure Databricks integrates with streaming sources like Azure Event Hubs and Apache Kafka for real-time data analytics. Use cases include fraud detection, recommendation engines, IoT analytics, and monitoring.

13.5.5 What are some of the machine learning frameworks and libraries that can be seamlessly integrated with Azure Databricks for advanced analytics?

Azure Databricks supports integration with popular machine learning frameworks such as TensorFlow, PyTorch, and XGBoost. It also offers built-in MLflow for model tracking and management.

13.5.6 How can Azure Databricks be used for time-series analysis and forecasting, and what tools and libraries are available for this purpose?

Azure Databricks provides tools and libraries like Prophet and ARIMA for time-series analysis and forecasting. Data scientists can leverage these to analyze historical data and make future predictions.

13.5.7 What is the role of Azure Databricks in automating machine learning workflows, and how does it simplify the process of model deployment and operationalization?

Azure Databricks streamlines machine learning workflow automation with MLflow and Azure Machine Learning integration. It simplifies model deployment, monitoring, and scaling, ensuring that machine learning models are production-ready.

13.6 Optimizing Performance and Scalability

13.6.1 How can organizations optimize the performance of Azure Databricks clusters for data processing tasks?

Organizations can optimize performance by selecting the appropriate cluster size, instance types, and node configurations based on workload requirements. Additionally, they should leverage cluster auto-scaling and dynamic allocation for resource efficiency.

13.6.2 What are some best practices for managing and monitoring cluster performance in Azure Databricks?

Best practices include using cluster logs and monitoring metrics, optimizing Spark configurations, and regularly reviewing and resizing clusters to match changing workloads.

13.6.3 How can data shuffling be minimized or avoided to improve query and job performance in Azure Databricks?

Data shuffling can be minimized by using techniques like bucketing, partitioning, and caching to reduce data movement between nodes, which significantly improves query performance.

13.6.4 What is the significance of Delta Lake's optimization features, and how do they enhance query performance and data consistency?

Delta Lake's optimization features include file compaction and Z-ordering, which improve query performance by reducing data access times and optimizing data layout. They also ensure data consistency and reliability.

13.6.5 How can Azure Databricks handle scaling out and managing clusters dynamically to accommodate varying workloads?

Azure Databricks offers cluster auto-scaling, which automatically adjusts the number of nodes in a cluster based on workload demand. This ensures that clusters can handle peak loads efficiently and scale down during idle periods to save costs.

13.6.6 Can you explain the role of data caching and broadcast variables in improving performance for frequently accessed datasets?

Data caching allows frequently used datasets to be stored in memory, reducing the need to recompute them in every job. Broadcast variables enable efficient sharing of small, read-only data across nodes, further improving query performance.

13.6.7 How does query optimization contribute to improved performance in Azure Databricks, and what techniques can be employed to enhance query efficiency?

Query optimization involves analyzing and restructuring SQL queries for better performance. Techniques include using appropriate indexes, optimizing joins, and avoiding unnecessary transformations, resulting in faster query execution.

13.7 Security and Compliance in Azure Databricks

13.7.1 What security features does Azure Databricks provide to protect data and workloads?

Azure Databricks offers a range of security features including data encryption in transit and at rest, Azure AD integration, role-based access control (RBAC), and network isolation to safeguard data and resources.

13.7.2 How does Azure Databricks ensure data compliance with industry regulations and standards?

Azure Databricks complies with various industry standards and regulations such as GDPR, HIPAA, and SOC 2. It provides features like audit logging and data residency options to support compliance efforts.

13.7.3 Can you explain the role of Azure Databricks Workspace and access controls in ensuring data security?

Azure Databricks Workspace is secured through Azure AD integration, allowing organizations to enforce authentication and access policies. Access controls, defined using RBAC, limit user permissions and data access to prevent unauthorized actions.

13.7.4 What is Azure Databricks' approach to data encryption, and how does it protect sensitive information?

Azure Databricks encrypts data at rest using Azure Storage encryption, and data in transit using TLS/SSL protocols. This dual-layer encryption ensures data remains secure both during storage and transmission.

13.7.5 How can organizations monitor and audit user activities and system events in Azure Databricks?

Azure Databricks provides audit logs that capture user activities and system events. These logs can be streamed to Azure Monitor or integrated with Azure Security Center for comprehensive monitoring and auditing.

13.7.6 What is the significance of network isolation in Azure Databricks, and how does it enhance data security?

Network isolation restricts inbound and outbound traffic, ensuring that Databricks clusters can only communicate with authorized resources. This prevents unauthorized access and enhances overall data security.

13.7.7 Can you explain how Azure Databricks helps organizations meet data residency and sovereignty requirements?

Azure Databricks offers multiple deployment options and data residency controls. Organizations can choose the Azure region where their data is stored and processed, helping them comply with specific data sovereignty requirements.

ONLINE RESOURCES

Practice Paper

Link : https://forms.gle/fnHtZorSYGvXEowV7

QR Code :

Video Content

Link : https://www.youtube.com/playlist?list=PLzlh_31VWEFoqaiFj8MjC35egoRca6TJu

QR Code :

Chapter 14: Miscellaneous Questions and Answers

Q 1. How is Azure different from AWS?

• Both Azure and AWS support hybrid cloud, whereas Azure supports hybrid cloud better.
• Azure offers express routes, while AWS offers direct connections.
• Azure has a virtual network cloud, whereas AWS has Virtual Private Cloud.

Q 2. Name three principal segments of Microsoft Azure.

• Windows Azure Compute: It provides a hosting environment for managed code and computation service through roles.
• Windows Azure Storage: It provides four types of Storage services - Queue, Tables, Blobs, and Windows Azure Drives (VHD).
• Windows Azure AppFabric: It provides five services - Service bus, Access, Caching, Integration, and Composite.

Q 3. Are you familiar with Azure CDN? If so, why is it important?

Yes, I'm familiar with Azure CDN (Content Delivery Network). Azure CDN is important for several reasons:
1. Global coverage- Azure CDN has over 200 points of presence (PoPs) in more than 90 countries, ensuring that content is delivered quickly and reliably to users worldwide.
2. Flexible caching- Azure CDN offers flexible caching options, allowing content to be cached at the edge or on the origin server. This can help reduce latency and improve performance for frequently accessed content.
3. Integration with Azure services- Azure CDN integrates seamlessly with other Azure services, such as Azure Storage, Azure Web Apps, and Azure Media Services.

Q 4. What is the difference between the Powerhouse and Repository Server?

Repository server controls the complete repository which includes tables, charts, and various procedures etc. Its main function is to assure the repository integrity and consistency. While a powerhouse server governs the implementation of various processes among the factors of server's database repository.

Q 5. What is your understanding of auto scaling in Azure?

Auto scaling in Azure refers to the ability of Azure services to dynamically adjust the number of compute resources based on current workloads and performance metrics. It ensures that applications and services can handle varying levels of traffic efficiently without manual intervention. Azure offers several auto scaling options, including vertical scaling (resizing VMs) and horizontal scaling (adding or removing VM instances), allowing organizations to optimize resource usage and cost while maintaining application performance and availability.

Q 6. Have you used the 'Migration Assistant' tool in Microsoft Azure?

We have successfully migrated 200 apps to Azure, while using the **App Service Migration Assistant** to migrate 60 different.NET Apps. The Azure Migrate App Service Migration Assistant really simplified our migration journey by identifying any migration blockers and enabling us to migrate apps with just a few clicks.

Q 7. While working on Azure, you encounter a drive failure. What will you do to solve the issue?

Below are the different steps which need to be performed when the drive failure occurs: -

1.First, we need to make sure that the Azure Storage will function without any fail, and we need to ensure that the drive is not mounted.

2.In another step we will replace the drive so that the drive gets remounted and formatted.

Q 8. Which service do you use to manage resources in Azure?

Azure Resource Manager is used to "manage" infrastructures which involve a no. of azure services. It can be used to deploy, manage and delete all the resources together using a simple JSON script.

Q 9. Can Azure availability set work with scale sets?

Yes, but there are some important considerations to keep in mind when using scale sets with availability sets. For more information, see the Azure documentation on the topic. One of the benefits of using scale sets with Azure availability sets is that the sets are automatically created when an availability set is created.

Q 10. How to stay current on Microsoft Azure?

To stay current with Azure, you can use the following resources[1]:

• Azure Service Health: Service Health alerts provide timely notifications about ongoing service issues, planned maintenance, and health advisories.

• Azure updates: Review Azure updates for announcements about product updates.

• Azure blog: The Azure blog communicates the most important announcements for the Azure platform.

Q 11. What service model in cloud computing do you know?

Cloud computing is offered in three different service models, each built to address specific business requirements. The three service models of cloud computing are:

1. Software as a Service (SaaS)
2. Infrastructure as a Service (IaaS)
3. Platform as a Service (PaaS)

Q 12. Have you ever used Windows Azure Compute Emulator?

By using Emulator Express, you can test and debug a cloud service without running Visual Studio as an administrator. You can set your project settings to use either Emulator Express or the full emulator, depending on the requirements of your cloud service.

Q 13. Do you have experience creating an HDInsight Cluster in Azure?

Azure HDInsight is a managed, full-spectrum, open-source analytics service in the cloud for enterprises. With HDInsight, you can use open-source frameworks such as, Apache Spark, Apache Hive, LLAP, Apache Kafka, Hadoop and more, in your Azure environment.

Q 14. Can you name different power states of a Virtual Machine?

There are seven power states that a VM can exist in:

Starting: Indicates that the VM is being started.

Running: Indicates that the VM is running.

Stopping: Indicates that the VM is being stopped.
Stopped: Indicates that the VM is stopped. Note that VMs in the stopped state still incur compute charges.
Deallocating: Indicates that the VM is being deallocated.
Deallocated: Indicates that the VM is completely removed from the hypervisor

Q 15. In your own words, define lookup transformation?
The Lookup transformation is a passive or active transformation used to look up data in a flat file, logical data object, reference table, or relational table. It is used to retrieve data based on a specified lookup condition. The Lookup transformation can return one row or multiple rows from a lookup.

Q 16. What do you know about the Azure Fabric Controller?
Azure Fabric Controller is the fundamental constituent incorporated in the configuration of Windows Azure and Windows Azure Service Platform, This fabric controller deals with the stipulation of hardware resources to the hosted software application. It administers the procedures of all hosted virtual equipment.

Q 17. Name a few Azure PaaS services.
Azure PaaS services include Web apps, Mobile apps, Logic apps, Functions, Web jobs, Service Fabric, and App Service Environment.

Q 18. Explain SQL Azure database.
Azure automatically handles patching, backups, replication, failure detection, underlying potential hardware, software or network failure, deploying bug fixes, failovers, database upgrades, and other maintenance tasks.

Q 19. Name four power states of a Virtual Machine.
1. Running: In this state, the VM is actively running and processing tasks. It's fully operational, and users can access and utilize its resources.
2. Stopped (Deallocated): When a VM is stopped and deallocated, it's completely powered off, and its resources are released. This state is cost-effective as users are not billed for the VM's compute resources when it's deallocated.
3. Stopped (Allocated): In this state, the VM is stopped but still allocated. While it's powered off, the VM's compute resources are reserved and billed, making it quicker to start again compared to deallocated state.
4. Paused: Some virtualization platforms allow VMs to be paused.

Q 20. Name two deployment environments offered by Azure.
• Dev Center Project Admin: Creates environments and manages the environment types for a project.
• Deployment Environments User: Creates environments based on appropriate access.

Q 21. What is Azure Data Lake?
Azure Data Lake is a highly scalable and secure data lake service provided by Microsoft Azure. It allows organizations to store and analyze vast amounts of structured and unstructured data, such as text, images, and logs. Azure Data Lake provides features like fine-grained access control,

analytics support with services like Azure Data Lake Analytics and Azure HDInsight, and seamless integration with Azure services, making it a powerful platform for big data storage and processing in the cloud.

Q 22. What is repetitive and minimal monitoring?

Repetitive and minimal monitoring" refers to a situation where a system or process requires very little ongoing attention or oversight due to its reliability and automation. In this context, repetitive tasks and routine checks are kept to a minimum because the system can handle most tasks independently. This term is often associated with well-designed and self-sustaining systems that minimize the need for human intervention, allowing operators to focus on more critical or exception-based activities.

Q 23. What is a hybrid cloud? Give four advantages of a hybrid cloud.

A hybrid cloud refers to a storage and computing infrastructure composed of a mixture of private cloud services, a public cloud, and/or on-premises infrastructure.

- Scalability: The hybrid cloud can adapt to the demands of each organization for space, memory, and speed.
- Control: The hybrid cloud gives businesses more control over their resource management and infrastructure.
- Speed: The hybrid cloud can reduce latency by optimizing infrastructure with edge computing.
- Security: The hybrid cloud can offer stronger security implementation and execution by combining private and public cloud solutions.
- Cost: The hybrid cloud can help organizations save costs in infrastructure and application support by presenting a more moderate initial investment.

Q 24. You have to synchronize all changes in the remote database with the SQL Azure database. How will you do it?

1. Login to the Azure Portal.
2. Browse the Azure SQL Server and Azure SQL database.
3. On the left blade, under the settings, locate the Data Sync service. Click Sync to other databases.
4. Follow the instructions to set up the sync group, add member databases, and add tables to the sync group1.
5. Replicate schema changes.

Q 25. What is hybrid and community cloud? Why are they both required?

A **hybrid cloud** is a combination of private and public cloud infrastructure, allowing data and applications to be shared between them. A **community cloud** is a cloud infrastructure shared by organizations with common interests or compliance requirements, like government agencies or industries.

Both are required for different reasons:

Hybrid Cloud: It offers flexibility, enabling organizations to leverage public cloud resources for scalability and cost-efficiency while maintaining sensitive data and critical applications in a private cloud. It's ideal for balancing performance, security, and cost considerations.

Community Cloud: It's needed when multiple organizations with similar needs must adhere to shared compliance or security standards. It provides a collaborative platform while ensuring data sovereignty and industry-specific requirements are met.

Q 26. What are the types of storage areas in Azure?

Azure Blob Storage: Ideal for storing unstructured data like documents, images, and videos. It's highly scalable and accessible via HTTP/HTTPS.

Azure File Storage: Provides file shares that can be accessed and managed like traditional file servers, making it suitable for SMB applications and sharing files across VMs.

Azure Table Storage: A NoSQL data store for semi-structured datasets like application logs and device information. It offers a schema-less design for flexible data storage.

Azure Queue Storage: Designed for reliable message queuing between components of cloud applications, enabling asynchronous communication and load leveling.

Azure Data Lake Storage: Optimized for big data analytics, it stores and analyzes structured and unstructured data at scale, with features like Delta Lake integration and data lakes for AI.

1. What is Microsoft Azure?

Answer: Microsoft Azure is a cloud computing platform that provides services such as virtual machines, storage, networking, databases, identity, monitoring, and security.

Reasoning: In interviews, Azure is best explained as a public cloud platform that helps organizations avoid buying and maintaining physical infrastructure. Instead of setting up servers manually, companies can create resources on demand. Azure supports IaaS, PaaS, and SaaS models. For administrators, Azure is important because they manage identities, subscriptions, governance, virtual networks, storage accounts, VMs, backups, and monitoring. A strong answer should show both definition and practical business value.

2. What are the main cloud service models in Azure?

Answer: The main cloud service models are IaaS, PaaS, and SaaS.

Reasoning: IaaS gives control over infrastructure such as VMs, disks, and networks. PaaS provides managed platforms such as Azure App Service, where developers deploy apps without managing servers. SaaS provides ready-to-use software such as Microsoft 365. Interviewers ask this to check whether you understand responsibility sharing. In IaaS, the customer manages more. In PaaS, Azure manages the platform. In SaaS, the customer mainly uses the application.

3. What is a Resource Group in Azure?

Answer: A Resource Group is a logical container used to manage related Azure resources.

Reasoning: Resource Groups help organize resources that share the same lifecycle. For example, a web app, database, storage account, and virtual network for one project can be placed in one Resource Group. Permissions, locks, tags, and policies can be applied at the Resource Group level. If the Resource Group is deleted, all resources inside it are deleted. This makes it important for cost management, access control, and administration.

4. What is an Azure Subscription?

Answer: An Azure Subscription is a billing and management boundary for Azure resources.

Reasoning: Every Azure resource must belong to a subscription. Subscriptions are used for billing, quotas, access control, and governance. Organizations often create multiple subscriptions for environments such as development, testing, and production. Azure RBAC can be applied at the subscription level. A good interview answer should mention that subscriptions sit below management groups and above resource groups in Azure's management hierarchy.

5. What is Microsoft Entra ID?

Answer: Microsoft Entra ID, formerly Azure Active Directory, is Microsoft's cloud-based identity and access management service.

Reasoning: Entra ID manages users, groups, applications, authentication, and access control. It supports features such as multi-factor authentication, conditional access, single sign-on, and identity governance. Azure administrators use it to control who can access Azure resources. In interviews, it is important to avoid saying Entra ID is exactly the same as traditional Windows Server Active Directory. It is cloud identity management, not a domain controller replacement.

6. What is Azure RBAC?

Answer: Azure RBAC stands for Role-Based Access Control. It is used to assign permissions to users, groups, service principals, or managed identities.

Reasoning: RBAC helps implement least privilege access. Permissions are assigned using roles such as Owner, Contributor, Reader, or specific service roles. RBAC can be applied at management group, subscription, resource group, or resource scope. Interviewers often ask RBAC questions to check if you understand access control. Owner can assign permissions, Contributor can manage resources but cannot grant access, and Reader can only view resources.

7. What is the difference between Owner and Contributor roles?

Answer: Owner has full access and can assign roles to others. Contributor can manage resources but cannot assign access.

Reasoning: This is a common Azure interview question because both roles allow resource management. The key difference is permission delegation. Owner can manage access through role assignments, while Contributor cannot. For security, Contributor is safer when users only need to create or manage resources. Owner should be limited to trusted administrators because it can grant permissions to other users.

8. What is Azure Policy?

Answer: Azure Policy is a governance service used to enforce rules and compliance standards across Azure resources.

Reasoning: Azure Policy can restrict allowed regions, require tags, block certain VM sizes, enforce encryption, or audit non-compliant resources. It is different from RBAC. RBAC controls what users can do, while Azure Policy controls what resources can be created or how they must be configured. For example, RBAC may allow a user to create VMs, but Policy can deny VM creation in unapproved regions.

9. What are Azure resource locks?

Answer: Azure resource locks protect resources from accidental deletion or modification.

Reasoning: Azure supports two main lock types: Delete and ReadOnly. A Delete lock allows users to read and modify resources but prevents deletion. A ReadOnly lock prevents modification and deletion. Locks can be applied at subscription, resource group, or resource level. They are especially useful for production resources. Interviewers may ask this to test your understanding of operational protection beyond RBAC.

10. What are Azure tags?

Answer: Tags are key-value metadata used to organize Azure resources.

Reasoning: Tags help with cost tracking, ownership, automation, and governance. Examples include Environment=Production, Department=Finance, or Owner=CloudTeam. Tags do not directly enforce security, but they are useful for reporting and management. Azure Policy can be used to require or inherit tags. In interviews, explain tags as an organizational and cost-management feature.

11. What is Azure Storage Account?

Answer: An Azure Storage Account is a container that provides access to Azure Storage services such as Blob, File, Queue, and Table storage.

Reasoning: Storage accounts are used to store different types of data. Blob Storage stores unstructured data like images and backups. Azure Files provides SMB/NFS file shares. Queue Storage handles messages. Table Storage stores NoSQL key-value data. Administrators configure redundancy, access keys, firewalls, encryption, private endpoints, lifecycle rules, and access tiers on storage accounts.

12. What is Blob Storage?

Answer: Blob Storage is Azure's object storage service for unstructured data.

Reasoning: Blob Storage is used for files such as images, videos, logs, backups, documents, and large datasets. It supports access tiers such as Hot, Cool, Cold, and Archive depending on usage frequency and cost needs. Interviewers ask this to confirm that you know which storage service fits which workload. Blob is best for object data, not mounted shared folders or relational databases.

13. What is Azure Files?

Answer: Azure Files is a managed file share service that supports SMB and NFS protocols.

Reasoning: Azure Files can be mounted as a network drive on Windows, Linux, and macOS systems. It is useful for replacing traditional file servers, sharing files across applications, and supporting lift-and-shift workloads. Unlike Blob Storage, Azure Files provides a true file share experience. Interviewers may ask this to check whether you can choose between Blob Storage and Azure Files.

14. What is a SAS token?

Answer: A Shared Access Signature token gives limited and time-bound access to Azure Storage resources.

Reasoning: SAS tokens are useful when you want to grant temporary access without sharing storage account keys. You can define permissions such as read, write, list, or delete and set expiry times. In interviews, mention that SAS follows the principle of least privilege. Account keys provide broad access, so SAS is usually preferred for temporary delegated access.

15. What is storage redundancy in Azure?

Answer: Storage redundancy controls how Azure replicates storage data for durability and availability.

Reasoning: Common options include LRS, ZRS, GRS, and GZRS. LRS replicates within one datacenter. ZRS replicates across availability zones in one region. GRS replicates to a secondary region. GZRS combines zone and geo redundancy. Interviewers often ask which option protects against datacenter or regional failure. For regional disaster protection, GRS or GZRS is required.

16. What is Azure Virtual Machine?

Answer: An Azure Virtual Machine is an IaaS compute resource that provides a virtualized server in Azure.

Reasoning: VMs are used when organizations need control over the operating system, software, networking, and configuration. Azure supports Windows and Linux VMs. Administrators manage VM size, disks, networking, availability, backups, patching, and monitoring. In interviews, mention that VMs provide flexibility but require more management than PaaS services like App Service.

17. What is an Availability Set?

Answer: An Availability Set distributes VMs across fault domains and update domains.

Reasoning: Availability Sets improve VM availability within a datacenter. Fault domains protect against hardware failures, while update domains protect during planned maintenance. However, Availability Sets do not protect against full datacenter failure. For datacenter-level protection, Availability Zones are better. This is a frequent interview comparison question.

18. What is an Availability Zone?

Answer: An Availability Zone is a physically separate datacenter within an Azure region.

Reasoning: Availability Zones provide high availability by isolating workloads across independent datacenters with separate power, cooling, and networking. If one zone fails, resources in another zone can remain available. Zones are useful for critical workloads requiring higher resilience. Interviewers often ask the difference between zones and sets: zones protect against datacenter failure, while sets protect against rack or maintenance failure.

19. What is a Virtual Machine Scale Set?

Answer: A Virtual Machine Scale Set lets you deploy and manage multiple identical VMs with autoscaling.

Reasoning: VM Scale Sets are used for scalable applications that need multiple VM instances behind a load balancer. They can automatically increase or decrease instances based on metrics such as CPU usage. This improves performance during high demand and reduces cost during low demand. It is commonly used for stateless web or application tiers.

20. What is Azure App Service?

Answer: Azure App Service is a PaaS service for hosting web apps, APIs, and mobile backends.

Reasoning: App Service allows developers to deploy applications without managing virtual machines. Azure handles infrastructure, patching, scaling, and platform maintenance. It supports languages such as .NET, Java, Node.js, Python, and PHP. Interviewers ask this to check your understanding of PaaS. Compared with VMs, App Service reduces administrative overhead.

21. What is Azure Virtual Network?

Answer: Azure Virtual Network is a private network in Azure used to connect Azure resources securely.

Reasoning: VNets allow resources like VMs, databases, and private endpoints to communicate using private IP addresses. VNets contain subnets and can connect to other VNets or on-premises networks. Administrators configure address spaces, subnets, NSGs, route tables, peering, VPN gateways, and private DNS. Networking is a major Azure interview topic.

22. What is a subnet in Azure?

Answer: A subnet is a smaller network segment inside a Virtual Network.

Reasoning: Subnets help organize and isolate workloads. For example, you can create separate subnets for web servers, application servers, databases, Azure Bastion, and gateways. NSGs and route tables can be associated with subnets. Proper subnet design helps improve security, routing, and scalability. Interviewers may ask subnetting questions to test real networking understanding.

23. What is a Network Security Group?

Answer: A Network Security Group is used to allow or deny inbound and outbound network traffic.

Reasoning: NSGs contain security rules based on source, destination, port, protocol, direction, and priority. They can be associated with subnets or network interfaces. Lower priority numbers are processed first. NSGs are a basic but critical Azure network security feature. They are not the same as Azure Firewall, which provides centralized and more advanced filtering.

24. What is VNet Peering?

Answer: VNet Peering connects two Azure Virtual Networks using private IP addresses.

Reasoning: VNet Peering allows resources in different VNets to communicate privately over Microsoft's backbone network. It can be regional or global. It is commonly used in hub-and-spoke architectures. Peering is low latency and does not require a VPN gateway. However, peering is non-transitive by default, so routing must be planned carefully.

25. What is Azure Monitor?

Answer: Azure Monitor collects and analyzes metrics, logs, and telemetry from Azure resources.

Reasoning: Azure Monitor helps administrators track performance, troubleshoot problems, create alerts, and visualize resource health. It integrates with Log Analytics, Application Insights, dashboards, and action groups. Interviewers ask about Azure Monitor because monitoring and maintaining resources is a key administrator responsibility. A good answer should mention both metrics and logs, because they are used differently for troubleshooting.

26. What is the difference between Azure Monitor Metrics and Logs?

Answer: Metrics are numerical data collected at regular intervals, while logs are detailed records of events and operations.

Reasoning: Metrics are lightweight and used for real-time monitoring, such as CPU percentage or disk usage. Logs, stored in Log Analytics, provide detailed diagnostic information and support advanced queries using KQL. Metrics are ideal for quick alerts, while logs are better for deep troubleshooting. Interviewers ask this to test understanding of monitoring strategies and when to use each type.

27. What is Log Analytics Workspace?

Answer: A Log Analytics Workspace is a centralized repository for collecting and analyzing log data.

Reasoning: It stores logs from Azure resources, on-prem systems, and other sources. Using KQL, administrators can query logs for troubleshooting, auditing, and performance monitoring. It integrates with Azure Monitor and Application Insights. Interviewers expect candidates to know that logs are not stored automatically without a workspace.

28. What is Azure Backup?

Answer: Azure Backup is a cloud-based service that protects data and workloads.

Reasoning: It allows backing up VMs, databases, and file shares to a Recovery Services Vault. It supports retention policies, scheduled backups, and restore options. Backup is critical for disaster recovery and business continuity. Interviewers often test knowledge of backup versus redundancy—backup protects from deletion, while redundancy protects from infrastructure failure.

29. What is Azure Site Recovery (ASR)?

Answer: Azure Site Recovery is a disaster recovery service that replicates workloads to another region.

Reasoning: ASR ensures business continuity during outages by replicating VMs and enabling failover. It supports planned and unplanned failovers. Unlike Azure Backup, which restores data, ASR keeps workloads running in another location. Interviewers often test the difference between backup and disaster recovery.

30. What is Azure Load Balancer?

Answer: Azure Load Balancer distributes network traffic across multiple resources.

Reasoning: It operates at Layer 4 (TCP/UDP) and ensures high availability by distributing traffic across backend VMs. It supports inbound and outbound rules. It is used within a region. Interviewers may compare it with Application Gateway, which works at Layer 7.

31. What is Azure Application Gateway?

Answer: Azure Application Gateway is a Layer 7 load balancer for web traffic.

Reasoning: It supports HTTP/HTTPS routing, SSL termination, cookie-based session affinity, and Web Application Firewall (WAF). It is used for web applications requiring advanced routing and security. Interviewers expect you to differentiate it from Load Balancer.

32. What is Azure Traffic Manager?

Answer: Azure Traffic Manager is a DNS-based global traffic routing service.

Reasoning: It routes users to the nearest or healthiest endpoint across regions. It supports routing methods like performance, priority, and geographic. Unlike Load Balancer, it works globally. Interviewers often test this distinction.

33. What is Azure Firewall?

Answer: Azure Firewall is a managed network security service that filters traffic centrally.

Reasoning: It provides application and network filtering rules, threat intelligence, and logging. It is typically deployed in a hub network. Unlike NSGs, it offers centralized control and advanced filtering.

34. What is Azure DDoS Protection?

Answer: It protects applications from Distributed Denial-of-Service attacks.

Reasoning: It automatically detects and mitigates large-scale attacks. Standard tier provides enhanced protection and telemetry. Interviewers expect candidates to know it works at the network edge.

35. What is Azure Bastion?

Answer: Azure Bastion provides secure RDP/SSH access via browser.

Reasoning: It eliminates the need for public IPs on VMs. It reduces attack surface and enhances security. Interviewers often ask this as a best practice for secure access.

36. What is a Private Endpoint?

Answer: A Private Endpoint connects Azure services privately using a VNet IP.

Reasoning: It ensures traffic stays within Azure's network. It improves security by avoiding public exposure. Commonly used for storage, SQL, and Key Vault.

37. What is Azure DNS?

Answer: Azure DNS is a hosting service for DNS domains.

Reasoning: It provides reliable domain name resolution using Microsoft infrastructure. It supports both public and private DNS zones.

38. What is Azure Key Vault?

Answer: Azure Key Vault stores secrets, keys, and certificates securely.

Reasoning: It provides controlled access, auditing, and integration with applications. It is essential for secure cloud design.

39. What is Managed Identity?

Answer: Managed Identity provides an automatically managed identity for Azure resources.

Reasoning: It eliminates the need to store credentials in code. Applications can authenticate securely to Azure services like Key Vault.

40. What is Azure Cost Management?

Answer: It helps track and control Azure spending.

Reasoning: It provides cost analysis, budgets, and alerts. Organizations use it to optimize cloud expenses.

41. What is Azure Advisor?

Answer: Azure Advisor provides recommendations for optimization.

Reasoning: It suggests improvements in cost, security, reliability, and performance. It is widely used for best practices.

42. What is Azure Policy vs RBAC?

Answer: RBAC controls access, while Policy enforces resource rules.

Reasoning: RBAC defines who can do what. Policy defines what can be deployed. Both are critical for governance.

43. What is Azure Automation?

Answer: Azure Automation automates repetitive tasks.

Reasoning: It uses runbooks (PowerShell/Python) to automate operations like patching and resource management.

44. What is Azure CLI?

Answer: Azure CLI is a command-line tool for managing Azure.

Reasoning: It allows scripting and automation. It is cross-platform and widely used by DevOps engineers.

45. What is PowerShell in Azure?

Answer: PowerShell is a scripting tool for Azure management.

Reasoning: It provides cmdlets for resource management. It is commonly used in automation and administration.

46. What is Azure DevOps?

Answer: Azure DevOps is a platform for CI/CD and software development.

Reasoning: It provides pipelines, repos, boards, and testing tools. It supports DevOps practices.

47. What is Infrastructure as Code (IaC)?

Answer: IaC is managing infrastructure using code.

Reasoning: Tools like ARM templates and Bicep allow repeatable deployments. It reduces manual errors.

48. What is Azure ARM Template?

Answer: ARM Template is a JSON file for deploying Azure resources.

Reasoning: It defines infrastructure declaratively. It ensures consistency and automation.

49. What is Bicep?

Answer: Bicep is a simplified language for ARM deployments.

Reasoning: It is easier than JSON and improves readability while providing the same functionality.

50. What is Azure SLA?

Answer: SLA defines uptime guarantees for Azure services.

Reasoning: It specifies availability commitments. Higher SLA requires proper architecture like zones or redundancy.

51. What is Azure NAT Gateway?

Answer: Azure NAT Gateway provides outbound internet connectivity for resources in a virtual network.

Reasoning: NAT Gateway allows VMs without public IPs to access the internet securely using a static public IP. It improves security by preventing inbound connections while enabling outbound communication. It also scales automatically and provides high availability. Interviewers often ask this to test understanding of outbound connectivity versus inbound access (handled by Load Balancer or public IP).

52. What is Azure VPN Gateway?

Answer: Azure VPN Gateway enables secure connectivity between on-premises networks and Azure.

Reasoning: It uses IPsec/IKE tunnels over the internet to establish encrypted connections. It supports site-to-site, point-to-site, and VNet-to-VNet connections. It is widely used in hybrid cloud environments. Interviewers may ask to differentiate it from ExpressRoute, which provides private connectivity.

53. What is Azure ExpressRoute?

Answer: ExpressRoute provides a private, dedicated connection between on-premises and Azure.

Reasoning: Unlike VPN Gateway, ExpressRoute does not use the public internet. It offers higher bandwidth, lower latency, and improved security. It is commonly used by enterprises with critical workloads. Interviewers expect candidates to know when to choose ExpressRoute over VPN Gateway.

54. What is Azure Disk Encryption?

Answer: Azure Disk Encryption protects VM disks using encryption.

Reasoning: It uses BitLocker for Windows and DM-Crypt for Linux to secure data at rest. It integrates with Azure Key Vault for key management. This ensures compliance and protects sensitive data. Interviewers often ask about encryption for security scenarios.

55. What is Azure Managed Disk?

Answer: Managed Disk is a disk storage service for Azure VMs managed by Azure.

Reasoning: Azure handles storage account management, scaling, and availability. It simplifies disk management compared to unmanaged disks. Managed disks also support different performance tiers like Standard and Premium SSD. Interviewers test this to check understanding of VM storage.

56. What is Azure Availability Set vs Availability Zone?

Answer: Availability Set protects within a datacenter, while Availability Zone protects across datacenters.

Reasoning: Availability Sets distribute VMs across fault and update domains. Availability Zones distribute resources across physically separate datacenters. Zones provide higher resilience. Interviewers frequently ask this comparison.

57. What is Azure Virtual Network Peering?

Answer: It connects two VNets using private IP communication.

Reasoning: Peering allows low-latency, high-speed communication without using VPNs. It supports global peering across regions. It is used in hub-and-spoke architectures. Interviewers test knowledge of network design.

58. What is Azure Route Table?

Answer: Route Table controls traffic routing within a VNet.

Reasoning: User Defined Routes (UDR) allow custom routing paths, such as directing traffic through a firewall. It overrides default system routes. Interviewers often include this in networking scenarios.

59. What is Azure Private DNS Zone?

Answer: It provides DNS resolution for resources within a VNet.

Reasoning: Private DNS zones allow internal name resolution without exposing services to the internet. They are often used with private endpoints. Interviewers expect candidates to understand internal networking concepts.

60. What is Azure Service Endpoint?

Answer: Service Endpoint allows secure connection to Azure services over Azure backbone network.

Reasoning: It extends VNet identity to Azure services like Storage and SQL. Unlike Private Endpoint, it still uses public endpoints but restricts access to specific VNets. Interviewers may ask to compare both.

61. What is Azure Blueprints?

Answer: Azure Blueprints allows deploying governed environments using templates.

Reasoning: It bundles policies, role assignments, and ARM templates into a single package. It ensures compliance and standardization across deployments. Though being replaced by deployment stacks, it is still relevant in interviews.

62. What is Azure Landing Zone?

Answer: A Landing Zone is a pre-configured environment for deploying workloads.

Reasoning: It includes governance, networking, identity, and security configurations. It ensures best practices for enterprise deployments. Interviewers may ask this in architecture discussions.

63. What is Azure Security Center (Defender for Cloud)?

Answer: It provides security management and threat protection.

Reasoning: It identifies vulnerabilities, enforces security policies, and detects threats. It gives recommendations and compliance insights. It is critical for securing cloud workloads.

64. What is Azure Sentinel?

Answer: Azure Sentinel is a cloud-native SIEM and SOAR solution.

Reasoning: It collects security data, detects threats, and automates responses. It integrates with Azure Monitor and Log Analytics. Interviewers ask this for security-focused roles.

65. What is Azure Application Insights?

Answer: Application Insights monitors application performance and usage.

Reasoning: It tracks requests, dependencies, failures, and user behavior. It helps developers troubleshoot performance issues. It is part of Azure Monitor.

66. What is Azure DevTest Labs?

Answer: It helps create development and testing environments quickly.

Reasoning: It allows developers to provision VMs with cost control policies. It reduces overhead in testing environments.

67. What is Azure Logic Apps?

Answer: Logic Apps automate workflows using connectors.

Reasoning: It enables integration between services without writing code. It is used for automation and integration scenarios.

68. What is Azure Functions?

Answer: Azure Functions is a serverless compute service.

Reasoning: It runs code in response to events without managing servers. It is cost-efficient and scalable.

69. What is Azure Container Instance (ACI)?

Answer: ACI allows running containers without managing infrastructure.

Reasoning: It is useful for short-lived or simple container workloads.

70. What is Azure Kubernetes Service (AKS)?

Answer: AKS is a managed Kubernetes service.

Reasoning: It simplifies container orchestration and scaling. Azure manages control plane components.

71. What is Azure Data Factory?

Answer: Data Factory is a data integration service.

Reasoning: It is used for ETL/ELT processes and data movement.

72. What is Azure Synapse Analytics?

Answer: Synapse is an analytics service combining big data and data warehousing.

Reasoning: It supports large-scale data analysis and reporting.

73. What is Azure Cosmos DB?

Answer: Cosmos DB is a globally distributed NoSQL database.

Reasoning: It provides low latency and multi-region replication.

74. What is Azure SQL Database?

Answer: Azure SQL Database is a managed relational database service.

Reasoning: It provides scalability, security, and automatic maintenance.

75. What is Azure Data Lake Storage?

Answer: It is a scalable storage service for big data analytics.

Reasoning: It supports hierarchical namespace and high-performance analytics workloads.

76. How do you secure access to Azure resources from the internet?

Answer: By using NSGs, Azure Firewall, WAF, private endpoints, and Azure Bastion.

Reasoning: Securing Azure resources requires a layered approach. NSGs filter traffic at subnet or NIC level. Azure Firewall provides centralized filtering. WAF protects web apps from attacks. Private endpoints remove public exposure. Bastion eliminates the need for public IPs for VM access. Interviewers expect candidates to demonstrate defense-in-depth strategy rather than relying on a single tool.

77. How do you ensure high availability for a web application in Azure?

Answer: Use Availability Zones, Load Balancer/Application Gateway, and Traffic Manager.

Reasoning: High availability requires redundancy across multiple layers. Availability Zones protect against datacenter failure. Load Balancer or Application Gateway distributes traffic within a region. Traffic Manager ensures global failover. Interviewers expect candidates to combine multiple services to achieve SLA targets rather than relying on a single feature.

78. How do you reduce Azure costs?

Answer: Use Azure Advisor, Cost Management, reserved instances, autoscaling, and right-sizing.

Reasoning: Cost optimization involves monitoring usage, eliminating unused resources, and selecting appropriate pricing models. Autoscaling reduces overprovisioning. Reserved instances provide discounts for long-term workloads. Advisor identifies underutilized resources. Interviewers expect practical cost-saving strategies, not just theory.

79. How do you implement disaster recovery in Azure?

Answer: Use Azure Site Recovery and Backup.

Reasoning: Disaster recovery ensures business continuity. Site Recovery replicates workloads to another region and enables failover. Backup allows data restoration. Together, they provide both operational continuity and data protection. Interviewers often test understanding of RTO (Recovery Time Objective) and RPO (Recovery Point Objective).

80. How do you monitor Azure resources effectively?

Answer: Use Azure Monitor, Log Analytics, alerts, and dashboards.

Reasoning: Monitoring requires collecting metrics and logs, analyzing them, and acting on alerts. Azure Monitor provides real-time metrics, while Log Analytics enables deep queries. Alerts notify administrators of issues. Dashboards visualize performance. Interviewers expect knowledge of proactive monitoring strategies.

81. What is the difference between Service Endpoint and Private Endpoint?

Answer: Service Endpoint secures public endpoints; Private Endpoint provides private IP access.

Reasoning: Service Endpoints extend VNet identity to Azure services but still use public endpoints. Private Endpoints assign a private IP inside the VNet, completely removing public exposure. Interviewers often ask this comparison to test network security understanding.

82. How do you design a secure Azure network?

Answer: Use segmentation, NSGs, Azure Firewall, private endpoints, and DDoS protection.

Reasoning: A secure network follows best practices like least privilege, segmentation, and layered security. Subnets isolate workloads, NSGs filter traffic, Firewall centralizes control, and private endpoints secure PaaS access. DDoS protection handles external attacks. Interviewers look for structured design thinking.

83. What is Zero Trust in Azure?

Answer: A security model that verifies every access request regardless of location.

Reasoning: Zero Trust assumes no implicit trust. It uses identity verification, least privilege, and continuous monitoring. Azure implements this using Entra ID, Conditional Access, MFA, and network controls. Interviewers expect conceptual understanding.

84. How do you implement identity security in Azure?

Answer: Use MFA, Conditional Access, RBAC, and Entra ID.

Reasoning: Identity is the first line of defense. MFA prevents unauthorized access. Conditional Access enforces policies. RBAC limits permissions. Entra ID manages identities. Interviewers expect layered identity security.

85. What is Conditional Access?

Answer: It enforces access policies based on conditions like location or device.

Reasoning: Conditional Access allows or blocks access depending on risk factors. For example, require MFA for external logins. It enhances security without affecting usability.

86. What is Azure Governance?

Answer: Governance ensures resources comply with organizational standards.

Reasoning: It includes Policy, RBAC, tags, and management groups. It controls cost, security, and compliance.

87. What is Azure Landing Zone architecture?

Answer: A structured environment for deploying workloads.

Reasoning: It includes networking, identity, security, and governance configurations. It ensures consistency and best practices.

88. What is Azure Hybrid Cloud?

Answer: Integration of on-premises and Azure resources.

Reasoning: It uses VPN Gateway or ExpressRoute for connectivity. It allows gradual migration and flexibility.

89. What is Azure Multi-region deployment?

Answer: Deploying resources across multiple regions.

Reasoning: It improves availability and disaster recovery. Traffic Manager handles routing.

90. What is Azure SLA design strategy?

Answer: Combine multiple services to meet uptime targets.

Reasoning: For example, use zones + load balancing + redundancy to achieve higher SLA.

91. How do you troubleshoot VM connectivity issues?

Answer: Use Network Watcher, NSG rules, and diagnostics.

Reasoning: Check NSG rules, routing, and VM status. Network Watcher provides tools like connection troubleshoot.

92. How do you secure storage accounts?

Answer: Use firewalls, private endpoints, encryption, and RBAC.

Reasoning: Avoid public access, use least privilege, and enable encryption.

93. What is Azure Defender for Cloud?

Answer: A security posture management and threat protection service.

Reasoning: It identifies vulnerabilities and provides recommendations.

94. What is Azure Arc?

Answer: It extends Azure management to on-prem and multi-cloud.

Reasoning: It allows managing non-Azure resources using Azure tools.

95. What is Azure Automation Runbook?

Answer: A script used to automate tasks.

Reasoning: It reduces manual work and ensures consistency.

96. What is Azure Backup vs Site Recovery?

Answer: Backup restores data; Site Recovery keeps workloads running.

Reasoning: Backup is for data protection, ASR is for disaster recovery.

97. What is Azure API Management?

Answer: A service for managing APIs.

Reasoning: It provides security, throttling, and monitoring.

98. What is Azure Event Grid?

Answer: Event-based messaging service.

Reasoning: It enables reactive programming using events.

99. What is Azure Service Bus?

Answer: Messaging service for communication between applications.

Reasoning: It ensures reliable message delivery.

100. What is the best way to prepare for Azure interviews?

Answer: Practice real scenarios, hands-on labs, and core concepts.

Reasoning: Azure interviews focus on practical knowledge, not just theory. Candidates should understand services, architecture, and troubleshooting. Hands-on experience is critical.

101. A VM cannot connect to the internet. How do you troubleshoot?

Answer: Check NSG rules, route tables, public IP/NAT Gateway, and DNS.

Reasoning: Start by verifying if outbound traffic is allowed in NSG. Then check route tables to ensure traffic is not misrouted. If the VM has no public IP, confirm NAT Gateway or Load Balancer outbound rules exist. Also verify DNS resolution. Interviewers expect a step-by-step troubleshooting approach rather than guessing a single issue.

102. A user cannot access a resource despite having Contributor role. Why?

Answer: Could be due to resource lock, policy restriction, or RBAC scope issue.

Reasoning: Contributor allows resource management but does not override locks or policies. A ReadOnly lock blocks changes. Azure Policy may deny operations. Also, RBAC might be assigned at a different scope. Interviewers test understanding of layered control systems.

103. How do you design a highly available VM architecture?

Answer: Use Availability Zones, Load Balancer, and VM Scale Sets.

Reasoning: High availability requires redundancy across zones and load balancing. Scale Sets provide automatic scaling. Combining these ensures SLA compliance. Interviewers expect multi-layer design thinking.

104. How do you secure communication between Azure services?

Answer: Use Private Endpoints, VNet integration, and encryption.

Reasoning: Avoid public endpoints, use private networking, enforce TLS encryption, and restrict access via RBAC. This ensures secure communication inside Azure.

105. A storage account is publicly accessible. How do you secure it?

Answer: Disable public access, enable firewall, use private endpoint.

Reasoning: Public exposure increases risk. Restrict access using network rules and private endpoints. Also use RBAC and SAS tokens for controlled access.

106. How do you implement least privilege access?

Answer: Use RBAC with minimal required roles.

Reasoning: Assign only necessary permissions at the lowest scope. Avoid Owner role unless required. Use custom roles if needed.

107. How do you enforce tagging across resources?

Answer: Use Azure Policy.

Reasoning: Policy can require or auto-apply tags. This ensures governance and cost tracking.

108. How do you monitor failed login attempts?

Answer: Use Azure Monitor and Entra ID logs.

Reasoning: Sign-in logs and audit logs help detect suspicious activity. Alerts can notify administrators.

109. How do you design cost-efficient architecture?

Answer: Use autoscaling, reserved instances, and right-sizing.

Reasoning: Avoid overprovisioning. Monitor usage and optimize resources regularly.

110. What happens if a region fails?

Answer: Use multi-region deployment with failover.

Reasoning: Deploy resources in multiple regions and use Traffic Manager or Front Door for failover.

111. How do you secure VM access without public IP?

Answer: Use Azure Bastion.

Reasoning: Bastion provides secure browser-based RDP/SSH without exposing ports.

112. How do you protect against data loss?

Answer: Use Azure Backup and replication.

Reasoning: Backup protects against deletion; redundancy protects against failure.

113. How do you detect security threats in Azure?

Answer: Use Defender for Cloud and Sentinel.

Reasoning: Defender identifies vulnerabilities; Sentinel provides SIEM capabilities.

114. How do you automate resource deployment?

Answer: Use ARM templates or Bicep.

Reasoning: Infrastructure as Code ensures consistency and repeatability.

115. How do you manage hybrid cloud connectivity?

Answer: Use VPN Gateway or ExpressRoute.

Reasoning: VPN is internet-based; ExpressRoute is private and high-performance.

116. How do you isolate workloads in Azure?

Answer: Use VNets, subnets, and NSGs.

Reasoning: Segmentation improves security and performance.

117. How do you control outbound traffic?

Answer: Use NAT Gateway and Firewall.

Reasoning: NAT provides outbound IP; Firewall controls traffic rules.

118. How do you ensure compliance?

Answer: Use Azure Policy and Blueprints.

Reasoning: Policies enforce rules; Blueprints standardize deployments.

119. How do you handle secrets in applications?

Answer: Use Azure Key Vault.

Reasoning: Avoid storing secrets in code; use secure retrieval.

120. How do you design scalable architecture?

Answer: Use VM Scale Sets, App Service, and autoscaling.

Reasoning: Scaling ensures performance during demand spikes.

121. How do you monitor network traffic?

Answer: Use NSG Flow Logs and Network Watcher.

Reasoning: These tools help analyze and troubleshoot traffic patterns.

122. How do you secure APIs in Azure?

Answer: Use API Management with authentication.

Reasoning: It provides throttling, security, and monitoring.

123. How do you implement disaster recovery for databases?

Answer: Use geo-replication and backups.

Reasoning: Ensures minimal data loss and quick recovery.

124. How do you troubleshoot performance issues?

Answer: Use Azure Monitor, metrics, and logs.

Reasoning: Identify bottlenecks using telemetry data.

125. What is the most important Azure interview tip?

Answer: Focus on real-world scenarios and hands-on experience.

Reasoning: Interviewers value practical knowledge. Understanding architecture, troubleshooting, and best practices is more important than memorizing definitions.

126. A VM is slow. How do you troubleshoot performance issues?

Answer: Use Azure Monitor metrics, check CPU, memory, disk I/O, and network usage.

Reasoning: Start with Azure Monitor to identify bottlenecks such as high CPU or disk latency. Then check VM size to ensure it matches workload requirements. Review disk type (Standard vs Premium SSD). Analyze network throughput. Also check if background processes or updates are consuming resources. Interviewers expect a structured approach—monitor → identify bottleneck → optimize resource.

127. How do you ensure secure data transmission in Azure?

Answer: Use HTTPS/TLS encryption and secure endpoints.

Reasoning: Data in transit must be encrypted using TLS/SSL. Azure services support HTTPS by default. Additionally, use private endpoints to avoid exposure to the public internet. Interviewers expect awareness of both encryption and network-level security.

128. How do you prevent unauthorized access to Azure resources?

Answer: Use RBAC, MFA, Conditional Access, and network restrictions.

Reasoning: Security is layered. RBAC controls permissions, MFA adds authentication security, Conditional Access enforces policies, and NSGs/firewalls restrict network access. A combination ensures strong protection.

129. How do you manage multiple subscriptions efficiently?

Answer: Use Management Groups.

Reasoning: Management Groups allow applying policies and RBAC across multiple subscriptions. They simplify governance in large organizations. Interviewers expect hierarchical understanding.

130. How do you optimize storage costs?

Answer: Use lifecycle management and appropriate storage tiers.

Reasoning: Move rarely accessed data to Cool or Archive tiers. Use lifecycle policies to automate this. Delete unused data. Interviewers expect cost-awareness.

131. How do you secure Azure APIs?

Answer: Use API Management with authentication and throttling.

Reasoning: API Management provides security, monitoring, and rate limiting. It protects APIs from abuse and ensures controlled access.

132. What is the difference between horizontal and vertical scaling?

Answer: Horizontal adds instances; vertical increases resources of one instance.

Reasoning: Horizontal scaling improves availability and is preferred in cloud environments. Vertical scaling is limited and may cause downtime. Interviewers expect cloud-native understanding.

133. How do you design fault-tolerant systems in Azure?

Answer: Use redundancy, zones, and load balancing.

Reasoning: Fault tolerance ensures system continues functioning despite failures. Use Availability Zones, replication, and load balancing. Interviewers look for resilience design.

134. How do you monitor application performance?

Answer: Use Application Insights.

Reasoning: It tracks response times, failures, and dependencies. It helps identify performance issues in applications.

135. How do you secure database access in Azure?

Answer: Use firewall rules, private endpoints, and RBAC.

Reasoning: Restrict access to trusted networks, use encryption, and avoid public exposure. Security is multi-layered.

136. How do you implement logging for compliance?

Answer: Use Azure Monitor and Log Analytics.

Reasoning: Logs help in auditing and compliance reporting. Store logs centrally and retain them as per policy.

137. How do you design a multi-tier application?

Answer: Use separate subnets for web, app, and database layers.

Reasoning: Segmentation improves security and performance. Each tier can have its own security rules and scaling.

138. How do you secure storage data at rest?

Answer: Use encryption.

Reasoning: Azure Storage is encrypted by default. You can use customer-managed keys for additional control.

139. How do you handle secrets in DevOps pipelines?

Answer: Use Azure Key Vault integration.

Reasoning: Avoid storing secrets in pipelines. Retrieve them securely from Key Vault.

140. How do you ensure application scalability globally?

Answer: Use Traffic Manager or Front Door.

Reasoning: These services route users to the best endpoint globally. They improve performance and availability.

141. How do you detect unusual activity in Azure?

Answer: Use Azure Sentinel.

Reasoning: Sentinel analyzes logs and detects threats using AI and analytics.

142. How do you restrict access based on user location?

Answer: Use Conditional Access policies.

Reasoning: You can allow/block access based on IP or geographic location.

143. How do you ensure backup reliability?

Answer: Use multiple recovery points and test restores.

Reasoning: Backup is only useful if it can be restored. Regular testing ensures reliability.

144. How do you design hybrid identity?

Answer: Use Azure AD Connect.

Reasoning: It synchronizes on-premises AD with Entra ID for unified identity.

145. How do you prevent accidental resource deletion?

Answer: Use Resource Locks.

Reasoning: Locks prevent deletion or modification of critical resources.

146. How do you manage updates for VMs?

Answer: Use Azure Update Management.

Reasoning: It automates patching and ensures systems are up-to-date.

147. How do you monitor network connectivity?

Answer: Use Network Watcher.

Reasoning: It provides tools like connection troubleshoot and packet capture.

148. How do you design secure DevOps pipelines?

Answer: Use least privilege, secrets management, and approvals.

Reasoning: Secure pipelines prevent unauthorized changes and protect credentials.

149. How do you implement role separation?

Answer: Use RBAC with different roles.

Reasoning: Separate duties among admins, developers, and auditors.

150. What is the key to success in Azure interviews?

Answer: Strong fundamentals + real-world scenarios + hands-on practice.

Reasoning: Interviewers focus on problem-solving and practical knowledge. Understanding how services work together is more important than memorizing definitions.

151. A web application is experiencing high latency. How do you troubleshoot?

Answer: Use Azure Monitor, Application Insights, and check network latency.

Reasoning: Start by analyzing metrics in Azure Monitor to identify CPU, memory, or network bottlenecks. Use Application Insights to trace requests and identify slow dependencies like databases or APIs. Check if the app is deployed in the correct region or if latency is due to geographic distance. Consider scaling resources or using CDN. Interviewers expect a layered troubleshooting approach rather than guessing a single issue.

152. How do you improve application performance globally?

Answer: Use Azure Front Door or CDN.

Reasoning: Azure Front Door provides global load balancing and caching, reducing latency by routing users to the nearest endpoint. CDN caches content closer to users. Together, they improve performance and user experience worldwide.

153. How do you secure communication between microservices?

Answer: Use private networking and TLS encryption.

Reasoning: Microservices should communicate over secure channels using HTTPS. Use VNets, private endpoints, and service-to-service authentication. Avoid exposing services publicly unless necessary.

154. How do you handle secrets in containerized applications?

Answer: Use Azure Key Vault and managed identities.

Reasoning: Containers should not store secrets in images. Managed identities allow secure access to Key Vault without credentials.

155. How do you ensure zero downtime deployment?

Answer: Use blue-green or rolling deployment.

Reasoning: Deploy new versions alongside existing ones and switch traffic gradually. This ensures continuous availability.

156. How do you monitor Kubernetes workloads?

Answer: Use Azure Monitor for containers.

Reasoning: It provides insights into node performance, pod health, and logs. Helps detect issues in AKS clusters.

157. How do you secure AKS clusters?

Answer: Use RBAC, network policies, and private clusters.

Reasoning: Restrict access, control network traffic, and avoid exposing API server publicly.

158. How do you design a secure multi-tenant application?

Answer: Use isolation, RBAC, and identity controls.

Reasoning: Each tenant must be isolated logically or physically. Use identity-based access and secure data separation.

159. How do you handle scaling in serverless applications?

Answer: Azure Functions auto-scale based on events.

Reasoning: Serverless automatically scales without manual intervention. It is cost-efficient and responsive.

160. How do you detect anomalies in Azure usage?

Answer: Use Azure Monitor and Cost Management alerts.

Reasoning: Alerts can detect unusual spikes in usage or cost. Helps prevent misuse or attacks.

161. How do you secure storage access from applications?

Answer: Use managed identities and RBAC.

Reasoning: Avoid using storage keys. Managed identities provide secure authentication.

162. How do you ensure compliance in Azure?

Answer: Use Azure Policy and compliance dashboard.

Reasoning: Policy enforces rules and provides compliance reporting.

163. How do you design disaster recovery for web apps?

Answer: Use multi-region deployment and Traffic Manager.

Reasoning: Deploy apps in multiple regions and route traffic during failure.

164. How do you optimize VM performance?

Answer: Choose correct VM size and disk type.

Reasoning: Match workload requirements with CPU, memory, and storage performance.

165. How do you secure API endpoints?

Answer: Use authentication, API Management, and throttling.

Reasoning: Prevent unauthorized access and limit abuse.

166. How do you manage identity lifecycle?

Answer: Use Entra ID governance features.

Reasoning: Automate onboarding/offboarding and access reviews.

167. How do you design network segmentation?

Answer: Use VNets and subnets.

Reasoning: Separate workloads for security and performance.

168. How do you implement logging strategy?

Answer: Use centralized logging with Log Analytics.

Reasoning: Store logs in one place for analysis and compliance.

169. How do you secure data backups?

Answer: Use encryption and restricted access.

Reasoning: Backup data must also be protected from unauthorized access.

170. How do you handle scaling for databases?

Answer: Use scaling options and replication.

Reasoning: Scale up/down or use read replicas for performance.

171. How do you monitor SLA compliance?

Answer: Use Azure Monitor and dashboards.

Reasoning: Track uptime and performance metrics.

172. How do you secure hybrid connectivity?

Answer: Use VPN or ExpressRoute with encryption.

Reasoning: Ensure secure communication between on-prem and cloud.

173. How do you design resilient storage?

Answer: Use redundancy like GRS or ZRS.

Reasoning: Protect data from failures.

174. How do you manage configuration drift?

Answer: Use Azure Policy and automation.

Reasoning: Ensure resources remain compliant.

175. What is the biggest mistake in Azure architecture?

Answer: Not designing for scalability and security.

Reasoning: Poor planning leads to performance issues, security risks, and high costs. Always design with best practices.

176. How do you design a highly secure Azure environment?

Answer: Use layered security with identity, network, and data protection.

Reasoning: A secure Azure design follows defense-in-depth. Start with identity security using Microsoft Entra ID, MFA, and Conditional Access. Then secure the network using NSGs, Azure Firewall, DDoS protection, and private endpoints. Protect data with encryption at rest and in transit. Monitor everything using Azure Monitor and Defender for Cloud. Interviewers expect a structured, multi-layered security approach rather than a single solution.

177. How do you troubleshoot DNS resolution issues in Azure?

Answer: Check DNS settings, private DNS zones, and VM configuration.

Reasoning: Ensure the VNet is linked to the correct DNS zone. Verify custom DNS settings if used. Check whether the resource is using Azure-provided DNS or custom DNS servers. Also validate NSG rules and routing. DNS issues often cause application failures, so interviewers expect a systematic troubleshooting approach.

178. How do you ensure secure access to web applications?

Answer: Use HTTPS, WAF, and authentication mechanisms.

Reasoning: Enforce HTTPS for encryption, use Application Gateway WAF for protection against attacks, and implement authentication using Entra ID or OAuth. This ensures both transport security and identity protection.

179. How do you optimize Azure networking performance?

Answer: Use accelerated networking, proper subnet design, and region selection.

Reasoning: Accelerated networking reduces latency and CPU overhead. Proper subnetting avoids bottlenecks. Deploy resources close to users to reduce latency. Interviewers expect knowledge of performance tuning techniques.

180. How do you implement high availability for databases?

Answer: Use geo-replication and failover groups.

Reasoning: Azure SQL and Cosmos DB support replication across regions. Failover groups ensure automatic switching during outages. This minimizes downtime and data loss.

181. How do you secure Azure storage accounts from public exposure?

Answer: Disable public access and use private endpoints.

Reasoning: Public endpoints expose data to risks. Use firewall rules and private endpoints to restrict access to trusted networks.

182. How do you design scalable web applications?

Answer: Use App Service or VM Scale Sets with autoscaling.

Reasoning: Scaling ensures performance during demand spikes. Combine with load balancing for reliability.

183. How do you monitor security posture in Azure?

Answer: Use Defender for Cloud.

Reasoning: It provides recommendations, vulnerability assessments, and threat detection. Helps maintain security compliance.

184. How do you handle identity federation?

Answer: Use Entra ID with external identity providers.

Reasoning: Federation allows users from other organizations to access resources securely without creating local accounts.

185. How do you design a cost-efficient storage strategy?

Answer: Use lifecycle management and appropriate tiers.

Reasoning: Move infrequently accessed data to Cool or Archive tiers automatically. This reduces storage costs significantly.

186. How do you secure VM access in production?

Answer: Use Bastion, Just-in-Time (JIT), and NSGs.

Reasoning: Avoid open ports. JIT provides temporary access. Bastion eliminates public exposure.

187. How do you implement logging for auditing?

Answer: Use Activity Logs and Log Analytics.

Reasoning: Activity Logs track administrative actions. Log Analytics stores detailed logs for analysis.

188. How do you design multi-region failover?

Answer: Use Traffic Manager or Front Door.

Reasoning: These services route traffic to healthy regions automatically during outages.

189. How do you secure APIs in Azure?

Answer: Use API Management with authentication and policies.

Reasoning: It enforces security, rate limiting, and monitoring.

190. How do you implement network isolation?

Answer: Use VNets, subnets, and NSGs.

Reasoning: Isolation prevents unauthorized access and improves security.

191. How do you handle large-scale data processing?

Answer: Use Azure Data Factory or Synapse.

Reasoning: These services handle ETL and analytics workloads efficiently.

192. How do you ensure application resilience?

Answer: Use redundancy and retry mechanisms.

Reasoning: Applications should handle failures gracefully and recover automatically.

193. How do you secure container workloads?

Answer: Use image scanning, RBAC, and network policies.

Reasoning: Prevent vulnerabilities and restrict access.

194. How do you manage secrets in applications?

Answer: Use Azure Key Vault.

Reasoning: Centralized secret management improves security.

195. How do you monitor cost anomalies?

Answer: Use Cost Management alerts.

Reasoning: Alerts detect unusual spending patterns early.

196. How do you implement hybrid networking?

Answer: Use VPN Gateway or ExpressRoute.

Reasoning: Provides secure connectivity between on-prem and Azure.

197. How do you ensure compliance reporting?

Answer: Use Azure Policy and compliance dashboard.

Reasoning: Provides visibility into compliance status.

198. How do you design microservices architecture in Azure?

Answer: Use AKS or App Services with API Management.

Reasoning: Microservices require scalability, isolation, and communication management.

199. How do you troubleshoot application downtime?

Answer: Use Azure Monitor, logs, and diagnostics.

Reasoning: Identify root cause using telemetry and logs.

200. What defines an Azure expert in interviews?

Answer: Strong fundamentals, hands-on experience, and problem-solving ability.

Reasoning: Interviewers prioritize practical skills, architecture design, and troubleshooting over memorization.

ADDITIONAL RESOURCES

Microsoft Azure Interview Q&A Videos Playlist-

Link: https://www.youtube.com/playlist?list=PLzlh_31VWEFoSFgM-EFhF2iD-q96w_rl8

QR Code:

All Microsoft Azure Certification Videos Playlist-
Link: https://www.youtube.com/playlist?list=PLzlh_31VWEFpyf3RWsfuUnS2lO3q1zlpj

QR Code:

Microsoft Azure Lab Practical Videos Playlist-

Link: https://www.youtube.com/playlist?list=PLzlh_31VWEFoRl74PavC9g71dYuy-Z8cP

QR Code:

Microsoft Azure MCQ Videos Playlist-

Link:
https://www.youtube.com/playlist?list=PLzlh_31VWEFpGrTXYHADZvN7aIH6YyGJZ

QR Code:

YouTube Videos Playlists for all Chapters

CHAPTER 1
Link : https://www.youtube.com/playlist?list=PLzlh_31VWEFoGhUkxGinUoUfYzHxGWEd6

QR Code :

CHAPTER 2
Link : https://www.youtube.com/playlist?list=PLzlh_31VWEFp3ynwA_kQilFAm8C5bzlue

QR Code :

CHAPTER 3
Link : https://www.youtube.com/playlist?list=PLzlh_31VWEFqWLxex3SQBEaVlhIJM74xi

QR Code :

CHAPTER 4
Link : https://www.youtube.com/playlist?list=PLzlh_31VWEFqYT2WoU09aJZ-dhNYmFtUr

QR Code :

CHAPTER 5
Link : https://www.youtube.com/playlist?list=PLzlh_31VWEFpFG3cjp6UwEkbUdTpT2w4e

QR Code :

CHAPTER 6
Link : https://www.youtube.com/playlist?list=PLzlh_31VWEFqZUZRBOTSPqmFPJtRYpCkQ

QR Code :

CHAPTER 7
Link : https://www.youtube.com/playlist?list=PLzlh_31VWEFrZl4Oy6kj5xVpSregtDO09

QR Code :

CHAPTER 8
Link : https://www.youtube.com/playlist?list=PLzlh_31VWEFooaIXkRIHSb-OLXUiyet6z

QR Code :

CHAPTER 9

Link : https://www.youtube.com/playlist?list=PLzlh_31VWEFqwP1IA7JXY-yFLLhCqXjN3

QR Code :

CHAPTER 10

Link : https://www.youtube.com/playlist?list=PLzlh_31VWEFofP0s7WR8xKlSnslKQj17G

QR Code :

CHAPTER 11

Link : https://www.youtube.com/playlist?list=PLzlh_31VWEFpFr6T1ebeeXHEAxVIr21B4

QR Code :

CHAPTER 12

Link : https://www.youtube.com/playlist?list=PLzlh_31VWEFpGxBhfZGwv4vpZFV2PjsMt

QR Code :

CHAPTER 13

Link : https://www.youtube.com/playlist?list=PLzlh_31VWEFoqaiFj8MjC35egoRca6TJu

QR Code :